Literature

and the Language Arts

Discovering Literature

UNIT ONE
RESOURCE

THE EMC MASTERPIECE SERIES

EMCParadigm Publishing Saint Paul, Minnesota

Staff Credits

Editorial

Laurie Skiba
Editor

Brenda Owens
Associate Editor

Lori Ann Coleman
Associate Editor

Diana Moen
Associate Editor

Gia Marie Garbinsky
Assistant Editor

Jennifer Joline Anderson
Assistant Editor

Janice Johnson
Curriculum Specialist

Paul Spencer
Art and Photo Researcher

Chris Bohen
Editorial Assistant

Chris Nelson
Editorial Assistant

Katherine S. Link
Editorial Assistant

Design

Shelley Clubb
Production Manager

C. Vern Johnson
Senior Designer

Parkwood Composition
Compositor

Cover Credits

Cover Designer: C. Vern Johnson

Saint George and the Dragon [**Detail**], c.1400s. Spanish Artist.
The Fate of Animals [**Detail**], 1913. Franz Marc.
Tornado Over Kansas [**Detail**], 1929. John Stuart Curry.

ISBN 0-8219-2032-4
© 2001 EMC Corporation

Published by EMC/Paradigm Publishing
875 Montreal Way
St. Paul, Minnesota 55102
800-328-1452
www.emcp.com
E-mail: educate@emcp.com

Printed in the United States of America.
10 9 8 7 6 5 4 3 2   XXX 02 03 04 05 06 07 08 09

Contents

Introduction iv

Selection Worksheet 1.1: "The Goodness of Matt Kaizer" 1

Selection Check Test 4.1.1 9

Selection Test 4.1.2 11

Selection Worksheet 1.2: "Eleven" 15

Selection Check Test 4.1.3 21

Selection Test 4.1.4 22

Selection Worksheet 1.3: "Why?" 25

Selection Check Test 4.1.5 33

Selection Test 4.1.6 35

Selection Worksheet 1.4: "Ta-Na-E-Ka" 38

Selection Check Test 4.1.7 48

Selection Test 4.1.8 50

Selection Worksheet 1.5: "The All-American Slurp" 54

Selection Check Test 4.1.9 63

Selection Test 4.1.10 65

For Your Reading List: Book Club 69

Unit One Review 70

Unit One Study Guide 73

Unit One Test 78

Supplemental Activity Worksheets 83

    Assignment Log 84

    Reader's Journal 85

    Research Journal 86

    Research Log 87

    Internet Research Log 88

Answer Key 89

Introduction

This introduction gives an overview of the unit resource materials available to you in teaching each unit. In using Unit Resource Books for units 2–12, you may want to refer back to this overview.

UNIT RESOURCE BOOKS

Each of the twelve units in LITERATURE IN THE LANGUAGE ARTS: DISCOVERING LITERATURE has its own Unit Resource Book. Each contains the following support materials, provided as reproducible blackline masters.

Selection Worksheets

Selection Worksheets include materials for all Reader Response and Teacher-Assisted activities for each literature selection. These include:

PREREADING

Daily Oral Language

Daily Oral Language activities provide two contextual sentences related to each literature selection in which students are asked to correct grammar, usage, and mechanical errors. While the Daily Oral Language exercises appear as part of the prereading materials, teachers may introduce them at any point in the lesson. Many instructors choose to start or end their class with these activities as a way to ensure continuing progress with language arts skill development.

Note: Additional practice in language, grammar, and style is provided throughout the program in literature post-reading exercises, in lessons integrated with the end-of-unit Guided Writing program, and in the Language, Grammar, and Style Resource in the Teacher's Resource Kit.

Reader's Journal

Reader's Journal activities relate the literature to students' experiences.

Graphic Organizers

Graphic organizers, important tools for visual learners, appear in prereading or post-reading materials, depending on when students are asked to use them in the textbook.

DURING READING

Guided Reading Questions

Guided Reading questions help students gather facts about the selection that will help in their response to higher-level thinking skills at the post-reading stage.

Art Smart questions

Art Smart questions throughout the textbook help students develop their visual literacy and critical viewing skills.

POST-READING

Respond to the Selection

Respond to the Selection activities relate the literature to students' lives.

Investigate, Inquire, and Imagine

Investigate, Inquire, and Imagine questions base literature interpretation on textual evidence.

Understanding Literature

Understanding Literature questions reinforce the literary concepts and techniques that were introduced on the Prereading page in the Reader's Toolbox feature.

Writer's Journal

Writer's Journal includes three quick-writing prompts that vary in difficulty.

Language Arts Skill Builder Worksheets

Language Arts Skill Builder Worksheets provide integrated activity worksheets based on the language arts activities that follow the literary selection. Additional Skill Builders worksheets are provided in Vocabulary and Language, Grammar, and Style.

Selection Check Tests

Each selection contains a selection check test that can be given as a quiz (graded or ungraded) to ensure that students have read the selection. Selection Check Tests include sections on Checking Your Reading (reading comprehension and vocabulary), and Reader's Toolbox (literary tools). Question formats vary and include multiple choice, true-false, matching, sentence-completion, and short answer items.

Selection Tests

Each selection contains a selection test that can be given after students have completed their study of the selection. Selection Tests include sections on Insightful Reading (comprehension, interpretation, and vocabulary), Understanding Literary Concepts, and Critical Writing (which include graphic organizers for visual learners and address higher-level thinking skills). Question formats vary and include multiple choice, true-false, matching, sentence completion, short answer, graphic organizer completion, and essay items.

Note: The numbering system of the Selection Check Tests and Tests reflects the organization of the Assessment Resource. The Assessment Resource Book contains all assessment materials for the program, except for Guided Writing, which has its own assessment tools in the Writing Resource Book. The Assessment Resource has four numbered parts: Part 1: Portfolio Assessment Forms; Part 2: Language Arts Survey Evaluation and Assessment Forms; Part 3: Comprehensive Tests: Language Arts Skills; and Part 4: Literature Selection and Unit Tests. All Selection Check Tests and Tests start with a number 4, followed by the unit number. Thus, Selection Check Test 4.1.1 for "The Goodness of Matt Kaizer" by Avi reflects the first selection in Discovering Literature, Unit 1.

End-of-Unit Materials

FOR YOUR READING LIST

The For Your Reading List feature at the end of each unit in the Pupil's Edition describes selections for independent reading and an accompanying activity. Blackline masters of the For Your Reading List activity are offered in the Unit Resource Book.

UNIT REVIEW

Each unit in the Pupil's Edition contains a Unit Review to help students prepare for the Unit Test. Blackline masters in the Unit Resource Book include all Unit Review materials from the textbook, including reviews of Words for Everyday Use and Literary Tools and a graphic organizer activity.

UNIT STUDY GUIDE

Each Unit Resource Book contains a Unit Study Guide to help prepare for the Unit Test. The Unit Study Guide includes a Vocabulary Worksheet that includes work with spelling and vocabulary skills such as synonyms, antonyms, analogies, context clues, and other vocabulary work; a Reader's Toolbox section that helps students review their understanding of literary tools spanning the unit; and Questions for Writing, Discussion, and Research, which allows them to apply higher-level thinking skills to their work within the unit.

UNIT TEST

The Unit Tests, like the Selection Tests, offer sections in Insightful Reading (reading comprehension, interpretation, and vocabulary), Understanding Literary Concepts, and Critical Writing (higher-level thinking questions). Question formats include multiple choice, true-false, matching, sentence completion, short answer, paragraph, graphic organizer, and essay items.

Additional Reading and Research Support in the Unit 1 Resource Book

ASSIGNMENT LOG

The Assignment Log is a blackline master that allows students to track their assignments throughout the course of study.

READER'S JOURNAL

The Reader's Journal is a reproducible page for keeping a journal or for responding to Reader's Journal prompts in the textbook.

RESEARCH JOURNAL

The Research Journal invites students to explore questions about topics they would like to investigate.

RESEARCH LOG

The Research Log gives students a framework in which they can chart their research.

INTERNET RESEARCH LOG

The Internet Research Log gives students a way to document and map their Internet research. It is particularly helpful for guiding students and remembering their path as they navigate through complex Internet sites and links.

ANSWER KEY

The Answer Key at the back of each Unit Resource Book provides answers to Daily Oral Language; Language Arts Skill Builders for additional vocabulary and language, grammar, and style activities not in the textbook; Selection Check Tests; Selection Tests; Unit Study Guides; and Unit Tests. The Annotated Teacher's Edition textbook provides answers for Guided Reading questions; Investigate, Inquire, and Imagine questions; Understanding Literature questions; and Language Arts Skill Builders. The Annotated Teacher's Edition also lists Selection Check Tests with answers.

ADDITIONAL SUPPORT BEYOND THE UNIT RESOURCE BOOKS

Guided Writing

WRITING RESOURCE BOOK

Each of the 12 units in the Pupil's Edition includes a Guided Writing assignment with an integrated Language, Grammar, and Style lesson. Full support materials in the Writing Resource Book include:

- Writing rubrics
- Guided Writing lesson worksheets
- graphic organizers
- student models
- alternative student models
- self- and peer evaluation checklists
- integrated Language, Grammar, and Style lesson worksheets
- assignment-specific rubrics

Writing Resource worksheets providing activities matched to the Writing Resource section in the Language Arts Survey. These worksheets survey the entire process of writing.

EMC MASTERPIECE WRITING: GUIDED WRITING INTERACTIVE SOFTWARE

The Guided Writing Interactive Software provides extended lessons that deliver print content and extensions electronically and includes a word process with features that simplify electronic composition and grading.

Teacher's Resource Kit

The Teacher's Resource Kit contains the following additional materials for you to draw from.

PROGRAM MANAGER

The Program Manager offers a complete map for adapting Literature and the Language Arts to your curriculum, student needs, and teaching style. The **Scope and Sequence** allows you to see the skills and activities the program covers, and the teaching resources the program provides. The **Lesson Planning Guide** allows you to choose from among the many activities available to build a complete lesson plan, whether you work with block scheduling or a more traditional classtime structure.

ASSESSMENT RESOURCE

The Assessment Resource Book contains all assessment materials for the program, except for Guided Writing, which has its own assessment tools in the Writing Resource Book (see Guided Writing Support, above). The Assessment Resource has four numbered parts: Part 1: Portfolio Assessment; Part 2: Language Arts Survey Evaluation and Assessment Forms; Part 3: Comprehensive Tests: Language Arts Skills; and Part 4: Unit and Selection Tests.

LANGUAGE ARTS RESOURCE BOOKS

Each of the following Language Arts Resource Books contains activities for additional practice beyond the activities in the textbook or Unit Resource Books. The Resource Books follow the numbering system of the Language Arts Survey in the textbook as follows:

1 Reading Resource
2 Writing Resource
3 Language, Grammar, and Style Resource
4 Speaking and Listening Resource
5 Study and Research Resource
6 Applied English Resource

There is at least one set of practice exercises for every numbered section in the Language Arts Survey. For example, the Language Arts Survey 1.1, "Purposes of Reading," introduces students to the concept that reading is done for a variety of purposes. Reading Resource worksheet 1.1, "Purposes of Reading," guides students through an activity based on this concept. If a teacher wishes to give students additional practice for the Language Arts Survey 3.31, "Correcting Sentence Fragments," the Language, Grammar, and Style Resource worksheet 3.31, "Correcting Sentence Fragments," provides ample opportunity for practice.

Supplemental Ancillaries beyond the Teacher's Resource Kit

VISUAL LITERACY/TRANSPARENCY RESOURCE

The Visual Literacy/Transparency Resource binder contains four-color, fine art transparencies and blackline masters of instructional material and activities that integrate the fine art throughout the program with the literature selections. The Visual Literacy component is designed to help students develop their critical viewing skills. Transparencies also include graphic organizers, student model drafts, and other work for students to do in whole-class activities.

AUDIO LIBRARY

The Audio Library includes 10 to 12 hours of audio recordings of the literature. The careful readings and dramatic intepretations are geared toward English language learners and auditory learners. They are also intended to motivate students by bringing to life the literature in the textbook.

Selection Worksheet 1.1

"The Goodness of Matt Kaizer"

DAILY ORAL LANGUAGE

Rewrite the following sentences, fixing any punctuation, grammar, spelling, or usage errors you may find.

Were going their tomorrow.

_____

"Did you see the way Karlyn looked at me," Joyce cryed.

_____

READER RESPONSE ACTIVITIES

Graphic Organizer

Use the graphic organizer below to note the details of Matt's character.

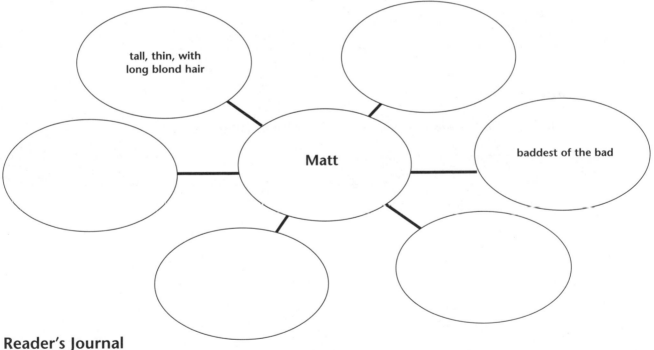

Reader's Journal

How do you react when someone dares you to do something?

_____

_____

_____

_____

Guided Reading Questions

PAGE 6

According to the narrator, what are the two important things to know about Matt Kaizer?

_____

_____

What is the gang always doing to Matt?

_____

_____

PAGE 8

What do Matt and his father disagree about?

_____

_____

What holds the gang together?

_____

_____

What does Marley dare Matt to do?

_____

_____

PAGE 9

What does Matt answer when Marley asks him what his father would say?

_____

_____

What does Matt decide to buy?

_____

_____

What does Marley whisper as they stand before the door?

_____

_____

PAGE 10

What lie does Matt tell Mary Beth?

_____

_____

PAGE 11

What is the worst thing about Mr. Bataky's appearance?

_____

_____

Who does Mr. Bataky think Matt is? What does he think Matt is going to do?

_____

_____

What does Mr. Bataky not want to do?

_____

_____

PAGE 12

What does Mrs. Bataky tell Matt's father? What does she ask him to do?

_____

_____

What does Rev. Kaizer dare Matt to do?

_____

_____

How does Mary Beth look at Matt when she opens the door?

_____

_____

PAGE 13

What does Mr. Bataky think will happen if he tells Matt all his bad stuff?

_____

_____

What does Mr. Bataky dare Matt to do?

_____

_____

Why won't Matt tell the others about the bad parts of Mr. Bataky's life?

_____

_____

PAGE 14

What's the only explanation Marley can give for Matt's change in appearance?

_____

_____

What does Matt think about how bad he is in comparison to Mr. Bataky?

_____

_____

What does Matt have to face?

_____

_____

RESPOND TO THE SELECTION

If you had been thinking about joining Matt's gang when Matt began to change, how would that have influenced your decision to join or not?

_____

_____

_____

_____

_____

_____

_____

INVESTIGATE, INQUIRE, AND IMAGINE

Recall

1a. Who in the story is the "baddest of the bad"? What kinds of things does he or she do?

_____

_____

_____

2a. What does Rev. Kaizer do when Matt says he doesn't want to go back to Mr. Bataky's?

_____

_____

3a. What nickname does the gang use for Matt? What does Mr. Bataky call Matt?

_____

_____

Interpret

1b. Why do you think the person is behaving this way?

_____

_____

_____

2b. What Rev. Kaizer does may seem a bit unusual for a minister. Why might he have done this?

_____

_____

3b. How are these names alike? What might be important about this?

_____

_____

Analyze

4a. What evidence can you find that Matt is not always being bad anymore?

_____

_____

_____

_____

Synthesize

4b. How do you think Matt will continue to change? Imagine a few possible situations that will help demonstrate your answer.

_____

_____

_____

_____

Evaluate

5a. To what degree did Mr. Bataky influence Matt? Explain your answer.

_____

_____

_____

_____

Extend

5b. Think of a time when someone caused you to change part of how you think about yourself. How did you feel at the time? How did your behavior change to match your new view of yourself? How do you feel about the experience now?

_____

_____

_____

_____

_____

UNDERSTANDING LITERATURE

CONFLICT. In "The Goodness of Matt Kaizer," someone besides the main character is struggling with conflict. Mr. Bataky is also struggling with something. What is his struggle, and is it internal or external?

_____

_____

_____

_____

CHARACTER. Fill in the chart below based on what you've learned about Matt throughout the story.

Matt	Physical Appearance	Clothing	Habits and Behaviors	Thoughts and Feelings
during first half of story:	• tall and thin • •	• • •	• watches MTV and cop shows • tells disgusting stories with buddies	• •
during second half of story:	•	• tie	•	• puzzlement

WRITER'S JOURNAL

1. Write a brief **note** to a classmate across the aisle that Marley might write to explain how the gang works.

_____

_____

_____

_____

_____

_____

_____

_____

2. Imagine that Mr. Bataky dies. Write a short **remembrance** about him that Matt might write in a sympathy card he's sending to Mary Beth and Mrs. Bataky.

_____

_____

_____

_____

_____

_____

_____

_____

_____

3. Imagine that Matt, in continuation of this story, is asking his father questions about the goodness in people. Write a short **dialogue** of two of Matt's questions and Rev. Kaizer's responses to each.

_____

_____

_____

_____

_____

_____

_____

_____

SKILL BUILDERS

Applied English

WRITING AN AD. Pretend you are Mrs. Bataky and you have just broken your leg in a bad fall. You need to advertise in the local paper for someone to assist you part-time in caring for Mr. Bataky. In as few words as possible, use the space below to write the ad, being sure to include the following information: description of job, days and hours needed, qualifications desired, and salary.

_____

_____

_____

_____

_____

_____

_____

_____

_____

_____

_____

Vocabulary

FORMING ADJECTIVES. *Sulky,* a Word for Everyday Use on page 12 of your textbook, is an adjective formed from the verb *sulk* by adding the suffix –*y.* Create new words by adding the suffixes shown to the following words. In general, when you add suffixes to words ending in *e,* the *e* is dropped.

1. beat + -able = _____

2. rasp + -ing = _____

3. admire + -able = _____

4. bite + -ing = _____

5. flush + -ed = _____

6. enjoy + -able = _____

7. stare + -ing = _____

8. fiction + -al = _____

9. climb + -able = _____

10. present + -able = _____

Language, Grammar, and Style

LOOKING AT SLANG. Slang is the informal, nonstandard vocabulary peculiar to a particular group. Such vocabulary, often temporary, consists typically of made-up or invented words, existing words that are used in new ways, and words that have been changed or exaggerated.

The author uses many slang words in "The Goodness of Matt Kaizer." Some of these words have been listed in the center column of the chart below. Look over these words and fill in their probable meanings. Then fill in the first column with slang that you've heard was popular in the past. Fill in the last column with slang (and their meanings) you and your friends use today. For fun, make up a few new slang words and their meanings for this column as well. Place a star by your inventions.

Slang used in the past		Slang used in the story		Slang used now (and in the future)	
word	meaning	word	meaning	word	meaning
		cool			
		neat			
		sweet			

- Of the slang words used in the past, which are still used today and which are no longer used?

  _____

  _____

- Of the slang words used today, which will probably be around for a while and which are being used less often or replaced by new slang?

  _____

  _____

- Which of all the slang words on the chart are your favorites?

  _____

  _____

Selection Check Test 4.1.1

"The Goodness of Matt Kaizer"

CHECKING YOUR READING

Short Answer

1. What is the gang's nickname for Matt?

   _____

   _____

2. What does Matt's father do for a living?

   _____

   _____

3. What does Mr. Bataky think Matt really is?

   _____

   _____

4. How does Matt's father persuade Matt to go back to visit Mr. Bataky?

   _____

   _____

5. How has Matt's physical appearance changed by the end of the story?

   _____

   _____

VOCABULARY IN CONTEXT

Sentence Completion

Fill in each blank below with the most appropriate vocabulary word from "The Goodness of Matt Kaizer."
You may have to change the tense of the word.

      leer   flushed   sulky   taunt   retreat   rasping   reputation

1. Marcel worked hard to maintain his _____ as a good student.

2. For weeks after Hannah got over her bronchitis infection, her voice remained _____.

3. The winning team's faces were _____ with exertion.

4. Even though he knew he deserved his punishment, Randal was _____ the whole time he was on restriction.

5. The coach yelled at his players after he caught them _____ the other team.

READER'S TOOLBOX

Sentence Completion

Fill in the blanks using the following terms. You may not use every term, and you may use some terms more than once.

conflict   external conflict   internal conflict   main character

plot   one-dimensional character   three-dimensional character

1. _____ are also called *flat characters* or *caricatures.*

2. The plot of a story centers on the main _____.

3. The most important person or animal in a literary work is called the _____.

4. When a character faces a struggle within himself or herself, he or she is experiencing

   _____.

5. _____ have many qualities, like real people do.

Selection Test 4.1.2

"The Goodness of Matt Kaizer"

INSIGHTFUL READING

Matching

Choose the letter of the character who fits each description.

        a. Matt Kaizer...

        b. Marley...

        c. Mary Beth...

        d. Mr. Bataky...

        e. Rev. Kaizer...

_____ 1. is the narrator of "The Goodness of Matt Kaizer."

_____ 2. is a sick person who believes in angels.

_____ 3. is "the baddest of the bad."

_____ 4. is a kind person who believes "there's goodness in everyone."

_____ 5. is a shy, sad person.

True or False

_____ 1. The narrator of this story is Matt Kaizer's friend.

_____ 2. Because Matt had light hair and skin and wore large white T-shirts, his friends called him "Casper."

_____ 3. Matt is the son of a minister.

_____ 4. Matt told his friends all of the "bad stuff" the sick man told him.

_____ 5. Matt was unhappy to discover that he was really good inside.

VOCABULARY IN CONTEXT

Sentence Completion

Fill in each blank with the most appropriate vocabulary word from "The Goodness of Matt Kaizer." You may need to change the tense of the word.

taunt   retreat   delirious   convulsive   bolt   rasping   sulky   imploring   ghastly

1. When the children heard the sound of the ice cream truck, they _____ out of the house.

2. In the scary movie I saw yesterday, the monster had a(n) _____ appearance.

3. The puppy fetched its leash and let out a(n) _____ bark, indicating he wanted to go for a walk.

4. After his surgery, my father was slightly _____ from the medication.

5. The path we were following in the woods seemed to disappear, forcing us to _____ and find a new path.

UNDERSTANDING LITERARY CONCEPTS

Short Answer

1. Describe one **internal conflict** faced by a character in "The Goodness of Matt Kaizer."

_____

_____

_____

_____

_____

2. Is the character of Matt Kaizer a one-dimensional character or a three-dimensional character? How do you know?

_____

_____

_____

_____

_____

CRITICAL WRITING

Essay

Choose *one* of the following prompts and write an essay. Complete *both* the Prepare to Write and Write sections of the prompt you choose. Use your own paper as necessary.

1. Cause and effect

PREPARE TO WRITE. In "The Goodness of Matt Kaizer," the fact that Matt "never refuses a dare" causes him to do many things he would prefer not to do. Also, many of the things Matt does affect him and other people. Use this chart to list a few causes and effects from the story.

Causes	Effects

WRITE. Write one paragraph that explains one cause and effect relationship from the story. You might choose to explain how Matt's actions affect him or how they affect others.

_____

_____

_____

_____

_____

_____

_____

_____

_____

_____

2. Good deeds

PREPARE TO WRITE. Think about a time when you helped another person. It could be as simple as helping a parent or guardian clean the house or as involved as Matt helping Mr. Bataky feel better. Why did you decide to help the person? How did your help make the other person feel? How did it make you feel? What did you learn from the experience? Jot down your answers to these questions.

_____

_____

_____

_____

_____

_____

WRITE. In a brief essay, tell about the time you helped someone else. Be sure to explore your answers to the questions above in your essay.

_____

_____

_____

_____

_____

_____

_____

_____

_____

_____

_____

_____

_____

_____

_____

_____

_____

Selection Worksheet 1.2

"Eleven"

DAILY ORAL LANGUAGE

Rewrite the following sentences, fixing any punctuation, grammar, spelling, or usage errors you may find.

Have you ever been to the White house?

_____

She don't want to grow older because she like being a kid.

_____

READER RESPONSE ACTIVITIES

Reader's Journal

When do you feel most grown up and able to handle anything? When do you feel young and unsure of yourself?

_____

_____

_____

_____

_____

Guided Reading Questions

PAGE 21

How does the narrator comfort her mother when the mother is sad and needs to cry?

_____

_____

Why does the narrator wish to be one hundred and two?

_____

_____

What does Mrs. Price do with the sweater?

_____

_____

PAGE 22

What does Rachel try to remember?

_____

_____

What does Mrs. Price say in front of the whole class?

_____

_____

Why does Rachel start crying?

_____

_____

What does Phyllis Lopez remember? What does Mrs. Price pretend?

_____

_____

Respond to the Selection

Describe your last birthday and how you felt about it.

_____

_____

_____

_____

_____

_____

_____

INVESTIGATE, INQUIRE, AND IMAGINE

Recall

1a. According to Rachel, what don't people understand about birthdays?

_____

_____

_____

2a. What does Mrs. Price hold up for the class to
see? What does she ask the class? How does
the class respond?

_____

_____

_____

Interpret

1b. Does Rachel feel older when she wakes up on
her birthday? Why, or why not?

_____

_____

_____

2b. Why does Rachel say "even if it belongs to me,
I wouldn't say so?"

_____

_____

_____

3a. What does Sylvia Saldívar say to Mrs. Price? How do Rachel and Mrs. Price respond?

_____

_____

_____

_____

3b. What does Rachel do when the sweater is placed on her desk? What does she try to remember to feel better?

_____

_____

_____

_____

4a. What does Mrs. Price tell Rachel to do with the sweater?

_____

_____

4b. Why does Rachel obey Mrs. Price?

_____

_____

Analyze

5a. Identify the words and actions of Mrs. Price that affect Rachel's day.

_____

_____

_____

_____

_____

_____

Synthesize

5b. Why might Mrs. Price do and say these things? Why does Rachel react the way she does?

_____

_____

_____

_____

_____

_____

Evaluate

6a. What do you think Rachel does after school on this day? What do you think she tells her parents about the day? How do you think her mood might change, if at all?

_____

_____

_____

_____

Extend

6b. If you had been in Rachel's position, what would you have done? How would you have acted if you were Mrs. Price?

_____

_____

_____

_____

_____

UNDERSTANDING LITERATURE

DESCRIPTION. What objects or actions in "Eleven" are described in detail? How do those descriptions contribute to the story?

_____

_____

_____

SIMILE. Find examples of simile in "Eleven" and note them in a graphic organizer like the one that follows.

Graphic Organizer

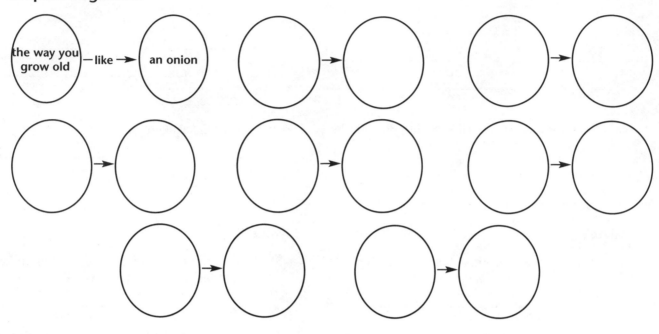

_____

WRITER'S JOURNAL

1. Imagine you are an advice columnist and that Rachel writes to you about the day of her eleventh birthday and about how she wishes she were older. Write a **letter of advice** back to her, expressing your thoughts.

   _____

   _____

   _____

   _____

   _____

   _____

   _____

   _____

2. Write three **similes** that compare items you own or see every day with other things.

   _____

   _____

   _____

   _____

   _____

3. Write a detailed **description** of a room in your home. Include details that appeal to all of the senses, revealing how things in the room look, sound, feel, smell, and taste.

_____

_____

_____

_____

_____

_____

_____

_____

Skill Builders

Language, Grammar, and Style

VERB TENSES: SIMPLE TENSES. Present tense shows that something is happening now. Past tense verbs talk about something that happened before now, and future tense verbs talk about something that will happen in the future. Look at the examples in the Language Arts Survey 3.61, "Simple Tenses." Then change the following present tense sentences to past and future tense.

1. Today I go for a walk.

   Yesterday _____

   Tomorrow _____

2. Today Raymond is studying with me.

   Yesterday _____

   Tomorrow _____

3. Today we are rehearsing.

   Yesterday _____

   Tomorrow _____

4. Today I do eat pizza.

   Yesterday _____

   Tomorrow _____

5. Today Mya teaches biology.

   Yesterday _____

   Tomorrow _____

6. Today Simon does run to the store.

   Yesterday _____

   Tomorrow _____

7. Today Anna meets Carrie at the library.

    Yesterday _____

    Tomorrow _____

8. Today Charlie is reading in front of the class.

    Yesterday _____

    Tomorrow _____

9. Today I see Tristin.

    Yesterday _____

    Tomorrow _____

10. Today Melania is eating a hot lunch.

    Yesterday _____

    Tomorrow _____

Vocabulary

USING A THESAURUS. Review the Language Arts Survey 5.21, "Using a Thesaurus." Next, use a thesaurus to find as many synonyms for the verb *age* as you can. Then write a paragraph explaining what *age* or *aging* means to you.

Synonyms for *age*:

_____

_____

_____

Paragraph explaining what *age* or *aging* means to you:

_____

_____

_____

_____

_____

_____

_____

_____

_____

_____

_____

_____

_____

Selection Check Test 4.1.3

"Eleven"

CHECKING YOUR READING

Short Answer

1. When you wake up on your eleventh birthday, what do you feel like?

   _____

   _____

2. What does Mrs. Price make the narrator wear?

   _____

   _____

3. How does the narrator describe this thing?

   _____

   _____

4. What does the speaker have to look forward to tonight?

   _____

   _____

5. What does the speaker wish would happen to this day?

   _____

   _____

READER'S TOOLBOX

Sentence Completion

Fill in the blanks using the following terms. Make the best choice for each question; you may not use every term, and you may use some terms more than once.

description   nouns   verbs   adjectives   adverbs   simile   sensory details

1. A _____ is a comparison using *like* or *as.*

2. Writers use _____, words or phrases that describe how things look, sound, smell, taste, or feel, to create description.

3. _____ is a type of writing that portrays a character, object, or scene.

4. The phrase " . . . it's hanging all over the edge like a waterfall" is an example of _____.

5. Effective description contains precise _____.

Selection Test 4.1.4

"Eleven"

INSIGHTFUL READING

Short Answer

1. What incident upsets Rachel on her eleventh birthday?

_____

_____

2. According to Rachel, why doesn't she stick up for herself to Mrs. Price?

_____

_____

3. Why does Rachel wish she was one hundred and two instead of eleven?

_____

_____

4. What does Rachel remember in order to make "the sick feeling" inside of her go away?

_____

_____

5. How does Rachel finally get rid of the red sweater?

_____

_____

UNDERSTANDING LITERARY CONCEPTS

Short Answer

1. What is a **simile?** Give one example of a simile. (You may use one from "Eleven," or you may create your own example.)

_____

_____

2. **Repetition** is more than one use of a sound, word, or group of words. Write one example of a word or a group of words that was repeated in "Eleven."

_____

_____

3. What kinds of elements help to create effective description?

_____

_____

CRITICAL WRITING

Essay

Choose *one* of the following prompts and write an essay. Complete *both* the Prepare to Write and Write sections of the prompt you choose. Use your own paper as necessary.

1. Your best birthday

PREPARE TO WRITE. In "Eleven," Rachel tells the story about one of her birthday experiences. Think about your birthday experiences. Which birthday comes to mind first? Is that your favorite birthday? What is your favorite birthday? What happened on that day? Who helped you celebrate your favorite birthday? Write your responses to these questions.

_____

_____

_____

_____

_____

_____

WRITE. In one to two paragraphs, write a memoir that tells the story of your favorite birthday. Be sure to tell what happened that day, who was involved, and why it is your favorite.

_____

_____

_____

_____

_____

_____

_____

_____

_____

_____

_____

_____

2. Summarize ideas

PREPARE TO WRITE. In "Eleven," Rachel shares many of her ideas about birthdays and growing older. Make a cluster chart to list and organize Rachel's ideas. Then think about whether you agree with her ideas.

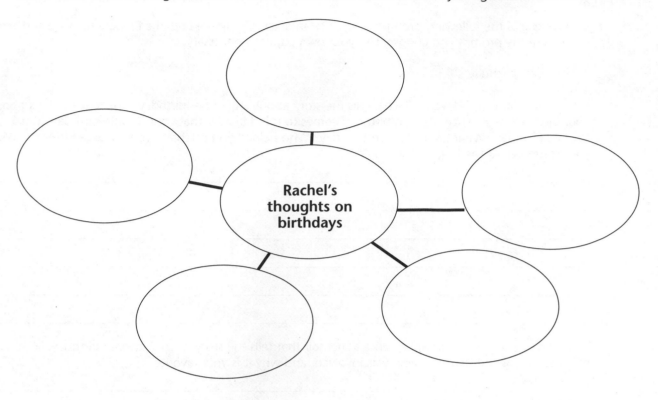

Rachel's thoughts on birthdays

WRITE. Write an essay about growing older. In the first part of your essay, summarize Rachel's ideas about growing older. In the second part, explain whether you agree with Rachel, and share some of your own ideas about growing older.

_____

_____

_____

_____

_____

_____

_____

_____

_____

_____

Selection Worksheet 1.3

"Why?"

DAILY ORAL LANGUAGE

Rewrite the following sentences, fixing any punctuation, grammar, spelling, or usage errors you may find.

Please tell you're dog to lay down.

_____

We seen the sillyest movie last night.

_____

READER RESPONSE ACTIVITIES

Reader's Journal

List the people who have been important teachers in your life. These people might be friends, family members, or school teachers. What have you learned about yourself and the world from these people?

_____

_____

_____

_____

_____

_____

Guided Reading Questions

PAGE 28

What was true of Anne Frank ever since she was a little girl?

_____

_____

What makes Frank believe that a person should ask "Why?" before doing something?

_____

_____

What does Frank believe that everyone has?

_____

_____

PAGE 29

Why might reasons be more effective than punishments?

_____

_____

What does Anne believe would make anyone better?

_____

_____

RESPOND TO THE SELECTION

How does Anne Frank believe that children should be raised? Do you agree? Why, or why not?

_____

_____

_____

_____

INVESTIGATE, INQUIRE, AND IMAGINE

Recall

1a. What was a "very strong thing" with Frank ever since she was a little girl? What does she say is a "well-known fact"?

_____

_____

_____

_____

2a. What did Frank realize about questions as she got older? What discovery did Frank make about questions that she did not feel she could ask or that she did not believe others could answer?

_____

_____

3a. According to Frank, what must a person ask of himself or herself before doing anything?

_____

_____

Interpret

1b. Why do children need to ask questions?

_____

_____

2b. What valuable skill did Frank learn by trying to answer her own questions?

_____

_____

3b. Why is it important for people to use this type of questioning?

_____

_____

4a. According to Frank, what should children do from their earliest youth? What does even a small child have?

_____

_____

_____

_____

4b. What does Frank believe should be encouraged and developed in children?

_____

_____

_____

Analyze

5a. What different points does Frank make about the word "why"? What different points does she make about asking questions?

_____

_____

_____

_____

_____

_____

Synthesize

5b. How can asking "why" and thinking things through for yourself make you a better person? How can it help to develop your conscience?

_____

_____

_____

_____

_____

_____

Evaluate

6a. Do you agree with Frank's statements about asking questions and learning? Why, or why not?

_____

_____

_____

_____

_____

Extend

6b. Think of a time in your life when you learned by asking questions. What did you learn? How might you learn something new today by asking questions?

_____

_____

_____

_____

_____

UNDERSTANDING LITERATURE

PERSONAL ESSAY. How do you know that Frank's essay is a personal essay? How does she relate her topic to her life?

_____

_____

_____

Graphic Organizer

Use the graphic organizer below to examine your thoughts about Frank's essay.

Topic _____	➤Thesis _____
	_____
	_____
	_____

Supporting Ideas
-
-
-
-

WRITER'S JOURNAL

1. Write a **topic sentence** that you could use for a personal essay. Then write a **list of questions** that your essay could answer or explore.

   Topic Sentence: _____

   _____

   Questions: _____

   _____

   _____

   _____

   _____

   _____

   _____

2. Write a **letter** to Anne Frank, telling her your thoughts about her essay and about asking questions.

   _____

   _____

   _____

   _____

   _____

   _____

   _____

_____

_____

3. Write **song lyrics** that use the word *why*.

_____

_____

_____

_____

_____

_____

_____

_____

SKILL BUILDERS

Applied English

RESPONDING TO INTERVIEW QUESTIONS. Imagine that you are interviewing for the position of tour guide for a student exchange program. Review the Language Arts Survey 4.1, "Verbal and Nonverbal Communication," and 4.7, "Communicating with Another Person." Then answer the following questions in the space provided. After you have finished, get together with a partner to practice responding orally to the questions.

1. Why did you respond to our job advertisement?

_____

_____

_____

_____

2. Why are you interested in this student exchange program?

_____

_____

_____

_____

3. Why do you feel you are the right person for the position?

_____

_____

_____

_____

4. Are you planning to pursue a career in tourism? Why, or why not?

_____

_____

_____

_____

5. In what field do you intend to pursue your education? Why?

_____

_____

_____

_____

6. Ask the interviewer three "why" questions about the organization or position.

_____

_____

_____

_____

LANGUAGE, GRAMMAR, AND STYLE

PRONOUNS. A **pronoun** is a word used in place of a noun. Two types of pronouns in the English language are the personal pronoun and the interrogative pronoun. Read the Language Arts Survey 3.41, "Using *I* and *Me*" and 3.52, "Types of Pronouns." Then underline the pronouns in each of the following sentences.

1. The little word "why" has been a very strong thing with me ever since I was a tiny little girl and couldn't even speak properly.

2. It is a well-known fact that little children ask questions about everything because they are unfamiliar with everything.

3. This was very much the case with me, but even when I grew older I couldn't wait to ask all kinds of questions, whether they could be answered or not.

4. This is not so terrible in itself and I must say that my parents tried to answer every one of my questions very patiently.

5. I console myself with the idea that there is a saying that says, "you must ask in order to know," which couldn't be completely true, otherwise I'd be a professor by now.

6. How would it be if everyone who did anything asked himself first, "Why?"

7. I can imagine that the last thing people like to do is to confess to themselves their faults and their bad side (which everybody has).

8. Most people think parents should try to educate their children and see to it themselves that their characters develop as well as possible.

9. By arguing reasonably and by showing the child the mistakes it is making, one would get much better results than by strong punishments.

10. The saying "you must ask in order to know," is true in so far as it leads to thinking about things, and by thinking nobody can ever get worse but will only get better.

Vocabulary

FORMING ADVERBS. *Reasonably* is an adverb formed from the adjective *reasonable,* a Word for Everyday Use on page 29 of your textbook, by adding the suffix *–ly.* Create new words by adding the suffix *-ly* to the following words.

1. nervous = _____

2. slow = _____

3. quiet = _____

4. thoughtful = _____

5. strong = _____

6. hurried = _____

7. obnoxious = _____

8. frequent = _____

9. frightful = _____

10. frigid = _____

Selection Check Test 4.1.5
"Why?"

CHECKING YOUR READING

Short Answer

1. Why do little children ask questions about everything?

_____

_____

2. The "little word 'why'" taught Anne not only to ask but also to do what?

_____

_____

3. People would become more honest and good if they did what?

_____

_____

4. What do both children and grownups hate to confess to themselves?

_____

_____

5. What is ridiculous by the time a child reaches the age of fourteen or fifteen?

_____

_____

VOCABULARY IN CONTEXT

Sentence Completion

Fill in each blank below with the most appropriate vocabulary word from "Why?" You may have to change the tense of the word.

    pedantic   conscience   character   reasonably   badger

1. Marcelle did the packing, because his wife was so _____ that it took her forever.

2. Priscilla's _____ bothered her so badly that she confessed what she had done.

3. Benjamin Franklin is remembered for working hard to develop his _____.

READER'S TOOLBOX

Matching

Match the best conclusion for each of the following statements.

a. expresses a writer's thoughts about a single subject.

b. relates to the life of the writer.

c. an introduction, a body, and a conclusion.

d. a single idea, or thesis.

e. the author's point of view.

_____ 1. A strong essay is organized into . . .

_____ 2. A personal essay is different from other types of essays because it . . .

_____ 3. A personal essay is written from . . .

Selection Test 4.1.6

"Why?"

INSIGHTFUL READING

True or False

_____ 1. Anne Frank explains that children ask questions only because they want to bother adults.

_____ 2. Frank believes "the little word 'why'" taught her both to ask and to think.

_____ 3. Frank learned that every question has an answer.

_____ 4. Frank believes that parents should be responsible for educating and developing the characters of their children.

_____ 5. Frank explains that punishment and spankings are useless once a child reaches age fourteen or fifteen.

VOCABULARY IN CONTEXT

Sentence Completion

Fill in each blank with the most appropriate vocabulary word from "Why?" You may need to change the tense of the word.

badger   character   conscience   reasonable   pedantic

1. Once the store manager understood that the customer's request was _____, he agreed to give her a refund.

2. My dad agreed to take us to the mall if we promised to stop _____ him about it.

3. Mateo's _____ told him that he shouldn't read his sister's journal, and he felt terrible after he did it.

UNDERSTANDING LITERARY CONCEPTS

Short Answer

1. How is a personal essay different from a regular essay?

_____

_____

2. From what point of view is a personal essay told? What words does the writer use in a personal essay that help readers understand the point of view?

_____

_____

3. What is a thesis? Into what three parts is a good essay organized?

_____

_____

_____

CRITICAL WRITING

Essay

Choose *one* of the following prompts and write an essay. Complete *both* the Prepare to Write and Write sections of the prompt you choose. Use your own paper as necessary.

1. Teaching children

PREPARE TO WRITE. In "Why?" Anne Frank offers her ideas about how children should learn. She also discusses the role that she thinks parents should play in their child's development. Use this cluster chart to record and organize Frank's ideas about how children learn. Now think about Frank's ideas and answer these questions: Do you agree with Frank's ideas about teaching children? What role do you think parents should play in a child's development? How do your parents or guardians help you grow and learn?

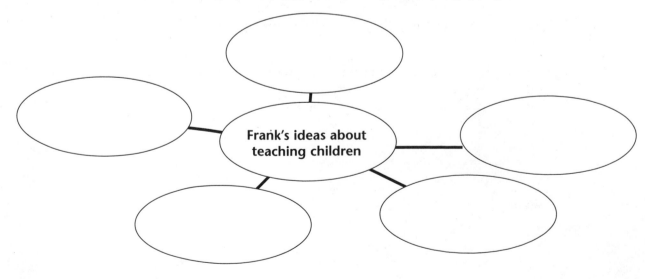

Frank's ideas about teaching children

WRITE. Write a one-page essay in which you compare your ideas about teaching children with Anne Frank's ideas. Include in your essay your thoughts about the questions above. If you disagree with Frank's ideas, explain why, and offer your own opinion on the subject.

_____

_____

_____

_____

_____

_____

_____

_____

_____

2. "Why?"

PREPARE TO WRITE. Anne Frank shares her opinion of "the little word 'why'" in this essay. Think about your opinion of the word *why*. What "why" questions did you ask when you were younger? Did you ever learn the answers to those questions? What "why" questions do you have now? How important is it to you that you learn the answers to those questions?

_____

_____

_____

_____

_____

WRITE. Create a two-stanza poem inspired by your thoughts about the questions above. In the first stanza, you might list several important "why" questions, and, in the second stanza, you might answer them. Or you might prefer to use your poem to share your opinion of "why" questions.

_____

_____

_____

_____

_____

_____

_____

_____

Selection Worksheet 1.4

"Ta-Na-E-Ka"

DAILY ORAL LANGUAGE

Rewrite the following sentences, fixing any punctuation, grammar, spelling, or usage errors you may find.

There was alot of geeses at the lake.

_____

"Can I stay out a hour later tonight" Peter asked?

_____

READER RESPONSE ACTIVITIES

Graphic Organizer

Keep track of the main events in "Ta-Na-E-Ka" by recording them in the graphic organizer below.

EARLY EVENTS:	The narrator is having nightmares about having to participate in Ta-Na-E-Ka.
MIDDLE EVENTS:	
MID-to-LATE EVENTS:	

Reader's Journal

What do you think about the traditions your family observes?

_____

_____

_____

Guided Reading Questions

PAGE 36

Why was eleven a magic word among the Kaws?

_____

_____

How did Mrs. Richardson suggest looking at Ta-Na-E-Ka?

_____

_____

What do most Kaw legends revolve around?

_____

_____

PAGE 37
How long was Ta-Na-E-Ka in Grandfather's boyhood, and what had to be done?

_____

_____

When Grandfather was a boy, which participants returned?

_____

_____

How long was Ta-Na-E-Ka for Mary and Roger, and what had to be done?

_____

_____

PAGE 38
How does Mary reply when Mrs. Richardson asks what she needs the five dollars for?

_____

_____

What couldn't Roger and Mary do during their Ta-Na-E-Ka?

_____

_____

PAGE 39
What did Mary realize as she watched a rabbit, a redheaded woodpecker, and a civet cat?

_____

_____

Why did Mary make sure the ladies' room window was unlocked?

_____

_____

PAGE 40
What did Mary take from the restaurant after it was closed for the night?

_____

_____

How does Mary respond to Ernie's reaction?

_____

_____

How does Mary feel after she puts on a loose sweater?

_____

_____

PAGE 41

What does Mary hope as she nears the door of her home?

_____

_____

How does Mary's grandfather look at her when she comes inside? How do Mary's uncle and aunt look at her?

_____

_____

What is Mary's reaction after she tells her grandfather what she learned about Ta-Na-E-Ka?

_____

_____

PAGE 42

What does Grandfather think about Mary's Ta-Na-E-Ka and her chances for surviving?

_____

_____

Respond to the Selection

Imagine you participated in a rite of passage like Ta-Na-E-Ka when you turned eleven, and describe what would have happened.

_____

_____

_____

_____

_____

_____

INVESTIGATE, INQUIRE, AND IMAGINE

Recall

1a. What are Mary's fantasies about?

_____

_____

_____

_____

2a. What is Mary's reaction when Ernie says Ta-Na-E-Ka is a "pretty silly thing to do to a kid"?

_____

_____

_____

_____

3a. How did Grandfather easily endure the entire period of his Ta-Na-E-Ka test?

_____

_____

_____

_____

Interpret

1b. What is she probably looking for in these fantasies?

_____

_____

_____

_____

2b. Why does she react this way when she herself had been thinking the same thing for months?

_____

_____

_____

_____

3b. What is similar about Mary's and Grandfather's experiences of Ta-Na-E-Ka?

_____

_____

_____

_____

Analyze

4a. Examine the events in the story that show Mary's careful honesty about money. Then examine the events that show her being dishonest about other matters—for example, her half-truths, lies, and sneaking actions. Rank the seriousness of her deceptions on a scale of one (least serious) to ten (most serious).

_____

_____

_____

_____

_____

_____

Synthesize

4b. What are the main causes for Mary's dishonest behavior? Why doesn't she feel guilty or uncomfortable about it?

_____

_____

_____

_____

_____

_____

Evaluate

5a. How effective is the author in creating a believable plot? How strong of a person does Mary seem to you, and why? To what extent, if any, did her making friends with Ernie impress Grandfather?

_____

_____

_____

_____

_____

_____

_____

Extend

5b. Tests of endurance occur throughout life in all cultures. What strategies and attitudes from the story would you choose to apply to the test you will face? Why do you think these strategies might work in more than one situation?

_____

_____

_____

_____

_____

_____

_____

UNDERSTANDING LITERATURE

DIALOGUE. What did you learn about Grandfather and his beliefs from what he says? What did you learn about Ernie and his beliefs? about Mary and her beliefs?

_____

_____

_____

_____

_____

_____

PLOT. What is the main conflict in "Ta-Na-E-Ka"? What part or parts of the story introduce you to the plot and characters? How do events within the middle section of the story help to develop the plot? How do events at the end of the story bring a conclusion to the story? How are problems or conflicts resolved at the end?

_____

_____

_____

_____

_____

_____

WRITER'S JOURNAL

1. Pretend you are Roger. Write a **diary entry** about some of the details and experiences of your five-day Ta-Na-E-Ka.

   _____

   _____

   _____

   _____

   _____

   _____

   _____

2. Imagine you are Mary in her sixties and you are training your granddaughter for her Ta-Na-E-Ka. Make an **outline** for your granddaughter that lists the topics you will cover in the training.

   _____

   _____

   _____

   _____

   _____

   _____

   _____

   _____

   _____

3. Imagine that you are an editor at a medium-sized newspaper. Write an **editorial** for the newspaper that explains your views on the value of taking wilderness survival training.

   _____

   _____

   _____

   _____

   _____

   _____

   _____

   _____

Skill Builders

Speaking and Listening & Collaborative Learning

DEVELOPING DIALOGUE. With a partner, develop and outline a dialogue between Mary and Roger describing and comparing the specifics of each of their Ta-Na-E-Kas. Record your dialogue below before you begin role-playing the conversation.

_____

_____

_____

_____

_____

_____

_____

_____

_____

_____

Collaborative Learning

RESEARCH: RESEARCH LOG. Use this log to keep track of the sources you use, the information you find, and your reactions to what you find when researching the transfer of Native American lands to the United States.

Books and print sources: _____

_____

_____

_____

_____

_____

_____

_____

_____

Name____________________ Class__________ Date__________

Internet sources: ____________________

Key Points: ____________________

Your reactions: ____________________

Language, Grammar, and Style

PARTS OF SPEECH. The *parts of speech* are: noun, verb, pronoun, adjective, adverb, preposition, conjunction, and interjection. Review the definitions and examples given for each part of speech in the Language Arts Survey 3.7, "Grammar Reference Chart—Parts of Speech Overview." Then, identify the part of speech of each underlined word in the sentences below.

EXAMPLE   Roger would <u>give</u> anything to get out of participating in <u>Ta-Na-E-Ka</u>.
give: verb; Ta-Na-E-Ka: noun

1. Many of the younger <u>families</u> on the <u>reservation</u> were beginning to give up the old customs.

   _____

2. <u>They</u> all advised us to fill up <u>now,</u> since for the next five days we'd be gorging ourselves on crickets.

   _____

3. He wore a sweat shirt with the words "Fort Sheridan, 1944," <u>and</u> he had only three fingers on one of <u>his</u> hands.

   _____

4. "I'll probably laugh about this when I'm an accountant," <u>Roger</u> said, <u>trembling</u>.

   _____

5. What if Grandfather <u>asks</u> me <u>about</u> the berries and the grasshoppers?

   _____

6 It never once <u>occurred</u> to me that being <u>Indian</u> was exciting.

   _____

7. It would have saved nights of bad dreams about <u>squooshy</u> grasshoppers.

   _____

8. He could speak English, <u>but</u> he spoke it <u>only</u> with white men.

   _____

9. "That's the <u>lost-and-found</u> closet," he <u>said</u>.

   _____

10. I sucked in my breath and blurted out the <u>truth</u>: "<u>Hamburgers</u> and milk shakes."

   _____

11. *Argh*! I <u>spat</u> it out.

   _____

12. Somehow, you know how to exist in a world <u>that</u> wasn't made <u>for</u> Indians.

   _____

Vocabulary

Write a new sentence for each of the Words for Everyday Use found on pages 36–41 of your textbook.

1. anticipate _____

_____

2. audacity _____

_____

3. dejected _____

_____

4. equate _____

_____

5. fend _____

_____

6. heritage _____

_____

7. hospitality _____

_____

8. hostility _____

_____

9. ordeal _____

_____

10. sacred _____

_____

11. shrewd _____

_____

12. skirmish _____

_____

13. unsightly _____

_____

14. virtue _____

_____

Selection Check Test 4.1.7

"Ta-Na-E-Ka"

CHECKING YOUR READING

Short Answer

1. What is "Ta-Na-E-Ka" a test of?

_____

_____

2. What movement did the author always think originated with the Kaw?

_____

_____

3. Where does Mary decide to spend her first night of Ta-Na-E-Ka?

_____

_____

4. How did Mary's cousin Roger look when he returned from his Ta-Na-E-Ka?

_____

_____

5. What had Grandfather eaten during his Ta-Na-E-Ka?

_____

_____

_____

VOCABULARY IN CONTEXT

Sentence Completion

Fill in each blank below with the most appropriate vocabulary word from "Ta-Na-E-Ka." You may have to change the tense of the word.

heritage   audacity   virtue   sacred   anticipated   fend   hospitality

1. In a Buddhist marriage ceremony, the couple drinks from a _____ bowl.

2. "It's time to see if he can _____ for himself," the ranger said as he let the eagle go.

3. Angela chose to investigate her family _____ for her research paper.

4. True courage is a _____ most of us don't know we have until it is tested in some way.

5. The townspeople extended warm _____ to the refugees.

READER'S TOOLBOX

Short Answer

1. Write a short dialogue (four to six lines) between two characters. The characters can be people you know or characters you make up.

_____

_____

_____

_____

_____

_____

_____

_____

2. What is the plot of this story?

_____

_____

_____

_____

_____

_____

_____

Selection Test 4.1.8

"Ta-Na-E-Ka"

INSIGHTFUL READING

Multiple Choice

_____ 1. What does "Ta-Na-E-Ka" mean to the Kaw Indians?
a. It is the word for "birthday."

b. It is a coming-of-age endurance test.

c. It is the word for "equality."

d. It is a method for understanding the modern world.

_____ 2. Roger Deer Leg, Mary's cousin, wants to be _____ when he grows older.
a. a warrior

b. a chef

c. an accountant

d. a writer

_____ 3. The Kaw Indians are a subtribe of the _____.
a. Sioux Nation

b. Omaha Nation

c. Seminole Nation

d. Flathead Nation

_____ 4. Mary and Roger were to spend _____ in the woods.
a. 3 days

b. 5 days

c. 14 days

d. 28 days

_____ 5. Mary spent her Ta-Na-E-Ka at _____.
a. a cabin

b. a church

c. a friend's house

d. a restaurant

Short Answer

1. How does Mary's grandfather show that he honors the old customs of the Kaw tribe?

   _____

   _____

2. What kinds of things did Grandfather teach Mary and Roger during their training?

   _____

   _____

3. How did Mary get five dollars for her Ta-Na-E-Ka?

   _____

   _____

4. What kinds of things do Ernie and Mary teach each other?

   _____

   _____

5. How does Mary's family react to the way she spent her Ta-Na-E-Ka?

   _____

   _____

VOCABULARY IN CONTEXT

Sentence Completion

Fill in each blank with the most appropriate vocabulary word from "Ta-Na-E-Ka." You may need to change the tense of the word.

   shrewd   ordeal   anticipate   dejected   unsightly   hostility   audacity

1. José was _____ when he learned that he did not get the lead role in the school play.

2. My classmates and I had _____ our field trip to the museum for weeks, and we were not disappointed by it.

3. The woman involved in the shipwreck was on the TV news explaining how she survived the

   _____.

4. The _____ businesswoman was successful because she was always able to find a solution to each problem she faced.

5. My sister looked at me with _____ when I told Mom that she was the one who broke the VCR.

UNDERSTANDING LITERARY CONCEPTS

Short Answer

1. Through **dialogue**, a reader learns a lot about the characters. What did you learn about Mary and Grandfather through their dialogue at the end of the story?

_____

_____

2. Define **plot**.

_____

_____

3. What is the central **conflict**, or struggle, in "Ta-Na-E-Ka"?

_____

_____

CRITICAL WRITING

Essay

Choose *one* of the following prompts and write an essay. Complete *both* the Prepare to Write and Write sections of the prompt you choose. Use your own paper as necessary.

1. Women's roles

PREPARE TO WRITE. The narrator of "Ta-Na-E-Ka" includes details about the history and customs of the Kaw Indians, particularly information relating to women. Record and organize the information in the selection that describes how women were treated in the Kaw tribe. Why did the Kaw stand out from other tribes in regard to their treatment of women? How are the Kaw customs different from how other cultures, including white cultures, treated women? (Remember that this story is set in 1947.) Do you think the way the Kaw Indians treated women was a good idea?

_____

_____

_____

_____

WRITE. Write an essay that summarizes roles Kaw women played in their culture. Conclude the essay by explaining your opinion of the Kaw customs. Use the questions above for guidance.

_____

_____

_____

_____

_____

_____

_____

_____

_____

2. The plot to a sequel

PREPARE TO WRITE. Mary Whitebird ends this selection by saying, "Grandfather wasn't entirely right. But I'll tell about that another time." What do you think happened to Mary later in her life? How do you think Mary handled other challenges she faced? Jot down a list of words that describe Mary's character. Then use your imagination to create a new challenge that Mary must overcome.

_____

_____

_____

_____

_____

_____

WRITE. Write a plot description for a sequel to "Ta-Na-E-Ka." Explain what challenge Mary will face next and how she will handle it. Make sure Mary stays true to her character; use your list of words that describe her character to guide you. Remember: You only have to explain the plot; you do not have to write the story.

_____

_____

_____

_____

_____

_____

_____

_____

_____

_____

_____

Selection Worksheet 1.5

"The All-American Slurp"

DAILY ORAL LANGUAGE

Rewrite the following sentences, fixing any punctuation, grammar, spelling, or usage errors you may find.

Are you a democrat or a republican?

_____

Their is many things that I do not understand about america.

_____

READER RESPONSE ACTIVITIES

Reader's Journal

What have you done when you were with new people and weren't sure of the correct eating procedures or manners?

_____

_____

_____

_____

_____

Guided Reading Questions

PAGE 48

How is raw celery different from cooked celery?

_____

What is the one problem with celery?

_____

PAGE 49

What does the narrator worry about when speaking English?

_____

PAGE 50

How does the father show off?

_____

What is another worry of the narrator?

_____

Why does the narrator "work on" her mother?

_____

PAGE 51

Why does Mrs. Lin want her daughter to borrow a girl's bicycle?

_____

What is the Lakeview restaurant like?

_____

What were two positive outcomes of Mr. Lin's promotion?

_____

PAGE 52

How does Mr. Lin prepare for the French menu?

_____

What is the correct way to eat soup according to the Chinese?

_____

What thoughts go through the narrator's mind as she looks in the mirror in the ladies' room?

_____

PAGE 53

What does Chinese etiquette force Mr. and Mrs. Lin to do when the teacher praises their daughter's progress?

_____

What do the Chinese use in place of large dinner plates?

_____

PAGE 54

What foods does Mrs. Lin serve at the dinner party?

_____

Why doesn't the narrator giggle when she and the others are watching the Gleasons eat?

_____

Respond to the Selection

If you had to move to a new country, learn a new language, and make all new friends, what do you think your main worries might be? What kinds of things would discourage you? What would help you along?

_____

_____

_____

_____

_____

_____

Art Smart

PAGE 48

In the picture on page 47, several items are exactly repeated. What does that suggest to you?

_____

_____

RELATED READING

"How to Eat Like a Child"

Additional Questions and Activities

PAGE 56

1. Name the two reasons peas are mentioned in the explanation of how to eat mashed potatoes.

   _____

   _____

2. In what order should you eat animal crackers?

   _____

3. Do any of these descriptions sound familiar to you? Do you use any of the suggestions listed here when you eat a particular food? If not, why? If so, which suggestions do you use?

   _____

   _____

   _____

   _____

INVESTIGATE, INQUIRE, AND IMAGINE

Recall

1a. What do the people in China do to all their vegetables before eating them?

_____

_____

2a. What does Mr. Lin say in the fancy restaurant after his wife says, "The French eat some rather peculiar things, I've heard"?

_____

_____

Interpret

1b. Why do you think they do this?

_____

_____

2b. What does Mr. Lin's response tell you about him?

_____

_____

3a. How does the Lin family eat their soup in the restaurant?

_____

_____

3b. Why might this behavior cause others in the restaurant to freeze and stare?

_____

_____

Analyze

4a. List the specific things the narrator worries about in this story.

_____

_____

_____

_____

_____

_____

Synthesize

4b. What is the biggest worry the narrator has but never talks about?

_____

_____

_____

_____

_____

_____

Evaluate

5a. In your opinion, how well is the Lin family adjusting to life in America?

_____

_____

_____

_____

_____

_____

Extend

5b. The related reading, "How to Eat Like a Child," also looks at ways to eat like someone else does, but the overall message is not the same as that in "The All-American Slurp." How do the messages differ?

_____

_____

_____

_____

_____

_____

UNDERSTANDING LITERATURE

THEME. What themes did you discover in "The All-American Slurp"? Which theme do you think is stressed the most? In what ways do the events support your choice?

_____

_____

_____

_____

_____

_____

ONOMATOPOEIA. List as many examples of onomatopoeia as you can.

_____

_____

_____

_____

_____

_____

WRITER'S JOURNAL

1. Imagine you are the narrator and you are writing a **postcard** to your best friend back in China. Tell your friend what you like most and least about living in the U.S.

_____

_____

_____

_____

_____

_____

2. Pretend you are the author of "How to Eat Like a Child." For future readers, write a **description** of how to eat one more food like a child.

_____

_____

_____

_____

_____

3. Write a personal **diary entry** that the narrator might write after finding out that all Americans slurp their milkshakes.

_____

_____

_____

_____

_____

_____

_____

SKILL BUILDERS

Language, Grammar, and Style

ONOMATOPOEIA. Words of onomatopoeia—like *splash, wow, gush, kerplunk*—are fun because they bring out the full flavor of words. Such words also make the meaning of the word much easier to understand, because an example is built right into the word. Find at least five examples of onomatopoeia in a comic book or the comic strip section of a newspaper and record them on the blanks provided below. Next, think of a high-action scene, such as a soccer game. Using the space provided below, write a description of your scene using as many onomatopoeia words as possible. If appropriate, use some of the words from the comics.

Examples:

1. _____
2. _____
3. _____
4. _____
5. _____

Description of your scene:

_____
_____
_____
_____
_____
_____
_____
_____
_____
_____
_____
_____
_____
_____
_____
_____
_____
_____
_____

Study and Research

RESEARCHING PEOPLE. Use the space below to write your master list of famous Chinese-Americans.

_____

_____

_____

_____

_____

_____

_____

_____

_____

_____

Speaking and Listening

IMMIGRATION INTERVIEW. Use the interview sheet below when you interview someone from another country.

Person's name:_____

Native country: _____

Immigration date: _____

Transportation used:_____

How long the trip took: _____

Special events of the trip:_____

_____

Special things brought along: _____

_____

Reasons person emigrated: _____

_____

_____

Who else came: _____

Arrival place in USA: _____

First USA sight:_____

First USA memory: _____

_____

_____

Language issues: _____

_____

Feelings about the move: _____

_____

_____

How USA is different from native land:_____

_____

_____

Any other notes of interest: _____

_____

_____

Vocabulary

ANTONYMS. An **antonym** is a word that means the opposite of another word. Find an antonym (or near antonym) for each of the following adjectives, or description words, from "The All-American Slurp." Use a dictionary or a thesaurus to check your answers or to help lead you to the answers. Once you have found antonyms for each word, use each antonym in a sentence.

EXAMPLE   common: rare

1. disgrace: _____

_____

2. retreat: _____

_____

3. revolting: _____

_____

4. sultry: _____

_____

5. systematic: _____

_____

Selection Check Test 4.1.9

"The All-American Slurp"

CHECKING YOUR READING

Short Answer

1. What clothes was Mrs. Lin at first reluctant to buy for her daughter?

   _____

   _____

2. Who was the narrator's first American friend?

   _____

   _____

3. What embarrassed the narrator at Lakeview Restaurant?

   _____

   _____

4. How did Mr. Lin react when his daughter's teacher praised her high grades at PTA?

   _____

   _____

5. What does Mr. Gleason do at the Lin's dinner party that surprises the narrator?

   _____

   _____

VOCABULARY IN CONTEXT

Sentence Completion

Fill in each blank below with the most appropriate vocabulary word from "The All-American Slurp." You may have to change the tense of the word.

ladled   favoritism   tense   sultry   revolting   unison   disgraced

1. The night was so _____ that we turned on every fan in the house.

2. Marcella liked many things about America, but she found fast food _____.

3. When the teacher called out the questions, the whole class answered in _____.

4. After some _____ moments, the Coast Guard ship pulled the survivor on board.

5. The team accused the coach of _____ when he gave his son the best position.

READER'S TOOLBOX

Sentence Completion

Fill in the blanks using the following terms. You may not use every term, and you may use some terms more than once.

emigrate   onomatopoeia   immigrate   theme

1. _____ is the use of words or phrases that sound like what they name.

2. A literary work may have several _____.

3. To _____ means *to arrive and settle in a new country or region.*

4. The Lin family _____ from China.

5. *Slurp, z-z-z-zip,* and *crunch* are examples of _____.

Selection Test 4.1.10

"The All-American Slurp"

INSIGHTFUL READING

Sentence Completion

1. The Lin family came to the United States from _____.

2. With the help of his new friends, the narrator's brother learned how to play _____ and earned a spot on his school team.

3. After the narrator rode a boy's bicycle, her mother agreed to buy _____ for her.

4. At the French restaurant, the narrator's family embarrassed her by slurping their _____.

5. After the Lins' dinner party, the narrator and Meg both get _____ from Dairy Queen.

Short Answer

1. Name one American custom the Lins learned at the Gleasons' dinner party.

_____

_____

2. What aspect of the English language fascinated Mr. Lin the most? Why?

_____

_____

3. Why did the Lin family decide to eat at the Lakeview Restaurant?

_____

_____

4. Why did Mr. Lin say that the narrator was a "stupid girl" when her teacher praised her?

_____

_____

5. Thinking about the narrator's embarrassment at the Lakeview Restaurant, how do you think she felt when Meg explained that "All Americans Slurp"?

_____

_____

VOCABULARY IN CONTEXT

Sentence Completion

Fill in each blank with the most appropriate vocabulary word from "The All-American Slurp." You may need to change the tense of the word.

sultry   mortified   spectacle   inflection   electronics   systematic   etiquette   residence

1. I was _____ to discover that I offended my guest by pronouncing his name incorrectly.

2. My mother told me to chew with my mouth closed, saying that I needed a lesson in proper _____.

3. My brother was recently hired at an _____ store, and he was learning a lot about radios and television sets.

4. Susan was _____ when doing her homework, always working on her math assignment first.

5. The football team created a _____ at school the day they showed up in cheerleader's uniforms.

UNDERSTANDING LITERARY CONCEPTS

Multiple Choice

_____ 1. Which of the following words is an example of **onomatopoeia?**
a. tickle

b. hiss

c. scream

d. bruise

_____ 2. Which of the following sentences might be considered a **theme** of "The All-American Slurp"?
a. In China, people do not eat raw vegetables.

b. The Gleasons lived next door to the Lins and invited them to a dinner party.

c. There are four people in the Lin family.

d. People must be patient and understanding when learning the customs and etiquette of other cultures.

CRITICAL WRITING

Essay

Choose *one* of the following prompts and write an essay. Complete *both* the Prepare to Write and Write sections of the prompt you choose. Use your own paper as necessary.

1. Defining America

PREPARE TO WRITE. When the Lins came to the United States, they learned about American culture. What do you think of when you think of American culture? Do you think about certain foods, sports, people, or customs? If the narrator asked you to tell her everything she needed to know to be an American, what would you tell her? What does the word *America* mean to you?

_____

_____

_____

_____

_____

_____

_____

_____

WRITE. Write one or two paragraphs explaining your ideas, or your definition, of America. Be sure to explain your ideas instead of just listing them.

_____

_____

_____

_____

_____

_____

_____

_____

_____

_____

_____

_____

2. Using onomatopoeia

PREPARE TO WRITE. Lensey Namioka uses onomatopoeia throughout "The All-American Slurp" to add humor and interest to her story. List some examples of onomatopoeia in the left column of this chart. Use the other column to explain each word. For example, you might write *tweet* and explain it as "the sound a bird makes."

Word	Explanation

WRITE. Write a poem or a short story that includes at least three examples of onomatopoeia. Make sure your examples of onomatopoeia illustrate the topic or subject of your poem or story.

_____

_____

_____

_____

_____

_____

_____

_____

_____

_____

_____

_____

_____

_____

_____

_____

_____

For Your Reading List

BOOK CLUB: DISCUSSION PROMPTS

You may want to jot down your own personal responses to these questions before meeting as a group.

- Where is this story set? Who are the main characters?

_____

_____

- What main conflicts does Cassie face? Are these conflicts internal or external? Explain.

_____

_____

- Is Cassie a well-developed character? In other words, does Cassie seem like a real person?

_____

_____

- What important lessons does Cassie learn by the end of the story?

_____

_____

- Do all of the issues and challenges Cassie faces seem believable? Why, or why not?

_____

_____

- Would you recommend this book to a friend? Why, or why not? To whom would you recommend it?

_____

_____

- Write one theme you discovered in *Roll of Thunder, Hear My Cry*.

_____

_____

Unit One Review

REVIEW: WORDS FOR EVERYDAY USE

Choose ten Words for Everyday Use from the unit list, and use each one in a sentence.

1. Word: _____

   Word in context: _____

   _____

2. Word: _____

   Word in context: _____

   _____

3. Word: _____

   Word in context: _____

   _____

4. Word: _____

   Word in context: _____

   _____

5. Word: _____

   Word in context: _____

   _____

6. Word: _____

   Word in context: _____

   _____

7. Word: _____

   Word in context: _____

   _____

8. Word: _____

   Word in context: _____

9. Word: _____

   Word in context: _____

   _____

10. Word: _____

    Word in context: _____

    _____

REVIEW: LITERARY TOOLS

Define each of the following terms, giving concrete examples when possible.

- character: _____

_____

- conflict: _____

_____

- description: _____

_____

- dialogue: _____

_____

- onomatopoeia: _____

_____

- personal essay: _____

_____

- plot: _____

_____

- simile: _____

_____

- theme: _____

_____

Graphic Organizer

For the main character of each selection in this unit, create a graphic organizer like this one. In the mirror, list what the character learned about himself or herself and about life in general. Compare the mirrors for each character. All together, what do these self-discoveries and life lessons have in common?

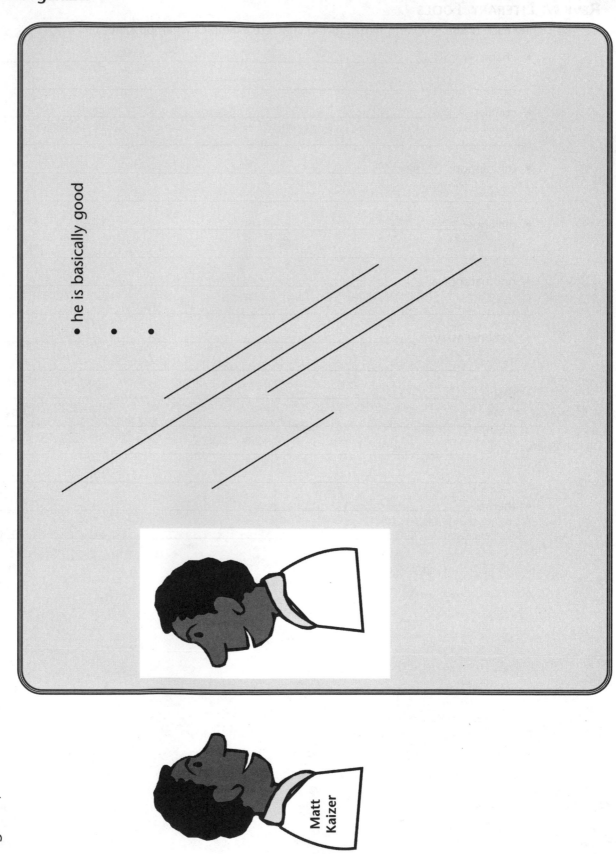

- he is basically good
-
-

Matt Kaizer

Unit One Study Guide

VOCABULARY WORKSHEET

Spelling

Circle the word that is spelled *incorrectly.* Then spell the word correctly on the blank provided.

1. _____

    a. flush

    b. ordeal

    c. discrace

    d. spectacle

2. _____

    a. bolt

    b. favoratism

    c. reasonable

    d. virtue

3. _____

    a. residence

    b. mordified

    c. pedantic

    d. shrewd

4. _____

    a. consciense

    b. unison

    c. ghastly

    d. equate

5. _____

    a. ladle

    b. systematic

    c. badger

    d. audasity

Synonyms

Choose the answer that comes closest to meaning *the same* as the underlined word.

1. Matt Kaizer was <u>dejected</u> when he learned that he was good inside.

   a. depressed

   b. confused

   c. exhausted

   d. relieved

2. The Lin family slowly learned American <u>etiquette</u>.

   a. laws

   b. phrases

   c. manners

   d. responsibilities

3. Roger's parents could not hide their <u>hostility</u> for Mary when she returned home.

   a. ill will

   b. pride

   c. respect

   d. jealousy

4. Mary had to be very <u>shrewd</u> in order to survive Ta-Na-E-Ka.

   a. mean

   b. courageous

   c. strong

   d. clever

5. Rachel might have been afraid her classmates would <u>taunt</u> her for wearing such an ugly red sweater.

   a. reject

   b. ignore

   c. tease

   d. congratulate

Antonyms

Choose the letter that comes closest to meaning *the opposite* as the underlined word.

1. Matt's experience with Mr. Bataky put him in a <u>sulky</u> mood.

   a. cheerful

   b. gloomy

   c. depressed

   d. lonely

2. Anne Frank believes children <u>badger</u> adults with questions because the children want to learn more.

   a. confuse

   b. bother

   c. honor

   d. delight

3. The narrator of "The All-American Slurp" was <u>mortified</u> when her family slurped soup at the expensive restaurant.

   a. proud

   b. angry

   c. embarrassed

   d. worried

4. Matt's friends wanted Matt to tell them all of Mr. Bataky's <u>ghastly</u> stories.

   a. frightening

   b. comforting

   c. unusual

   d. interesting

5. The Lins thought sour cream was a <u>revolting</u> food because they were not used to dairy products.

   a. clever

   b. expensive

   c. disgusting

   d. appealing

Sentence Completion

Fill in each blank with the most appropriate word from the following Words for Everyday Use from Unit One. You may have to change the tense of the word.

conscience   ordeal   favoritism   hospitality   unison   pedantic   reputation   spectacle

1. During her Ta-Na-E-Ka, Mary accepted the _____ offered by Ernie.

2. The Lins shook their heads in _____ when they were offered sour cream.

3. I hope Rachel's _____ with the red sweater did not ruin her birthday celebration at home.

4. Matt had a _____ for being the "baddest of the bad."

5. Anne Frank believes that a child's _____ will punish them if they act improperly.

READER'S TOOLBOX

Fill in the blanks using the following terms. You may not use every term, and you may use some terms more than once.

dialogue   simile   plot   personal essay   theme   onomatopoeia   conflict   character

1. _____ is the use of words or phrases that sound like what they name.

2. In a _____, a writer expresses his or her thoughts about a subject that relates his or her life.

3. A comparison using *like* or *as* is called a _____.

4. _____ is a struggle between two people or things in a literary work.

5. A _____ is a central idea in a literary work.

QUESTIONS FOR WRITING, DISCUSSION, AND RESEARCH

1. In "The Goodness of Matt Kaizer," Matt learns that he is not the person he thought he was. What discovery about himself does he make? What makes him come to this realization? What other characters in the unit go through difficult times before they learn something about themselves? Compare and contrast one other character's journey to self-understanding with Matt's experience.

_____

_____

_____

_____

_____

_____

_____

_____

_____

_____

_____

_____

_____

_____

_____

_____

2. Many of the selections in this unit feature characters who are trying to win the acceptance of other people. Choose one character and explain how he or she tries to gain acceptance from other people, why he or she wants this acceptance, and whether the character ever found the acceptance he or she desired. You might write about your ideas or discuss them in small groups.

_____

_____

_____

_____

_____

_____

_____

_____

_____

_____

_____

_____

_____

_____

_____

_____

_____

_____

_____

Unit One Test

INSIGHTFUL READING

Matching

Choose the letter of the character who fits each description.

　　　　a. Matt Kaizer...

　　　　b. Rachel...

　　　　c. Mary...

　　　　d. The narrator of "The All-American Slurp"...

_____ 1. thinks that growing older does not happen quickly enough.

_____ 2. helps a sick man feel better.

_____ 3. learns that people need time to get used to a new culture.

_____ 4. learns that there is good inside everyone, even "the baddest of the bad."

_____ 5. uses creativity to prove that she can survive a difficult test.

True or False

_____ 1. In "Why?" Anne Frank explains that children should try to educate themselves and build their own characters.

_____ 2. The Lin Family recently moved to the United States from Korea and are trying to learn American customs.

_____ 3. Roger and Mary were excited to participate in Ta-Na-E-Ka and could not wait until it began.

_____ 4. Rachel's teacher upset her on her eleventh birthday by making Rachel wear a red sweater that was not hers.

_____ 5. Matt Kaizer used his goodness to help his father recover from a serious illness.

VOCABULARY IN CONTEXT

Sentence Completion

Fill in each blank below with the most appropriate vocabulary word from Unit One. You may have to change the tense of the word.

leer   rasping   reputation   virtue   flush   consumption   favoritism   anticipate   disgrace

1. My mother always tells me that honesty is a _____ that will help me make many friends.

2. Katrina's face was _____ when she read her speech in front of the entire school body.

3. I think the candidate _____ himself during the debate by insulting his opponent.

4. My parents do not show _____ because they treat me and my siblings equally.

5. The two boxers _____ at each other as they entered the boxing ring.

UNDERSTANDING LITERARY CONCEPTS

Short Answer

1. What is *onomatopoeia?* Give one example of onomatopoeia that was included in "The All-American Slurp."

   _____

   _____

2. Which selection from Unit One is an example of a *personal essay?*

   _____

   _____

3. Give one example of a *conflict* experienced by one of the characters in "The Goodness of Matt Kaizer."

   _____

   _____

4. Which selection from Unit One includes a *simile* that compares growing old to an onion?

   _____

   _____

5. Identify one *theme* of "Ta-Na-E-Ka."

   _____

   _____

CRITICAL WRITING

Short Answer

1. How did Matt Kaizer's experience with Mr. Bataky help him realize that he had good inside him?

_____

_____

2. What do readers learn about Rachel's character from the fact that she did not stand up for herself with Mrs. Price?

_____

_____

3. Which aspects of "Why?" illustrate that the selection is a personal essay?

_____

_____

4. How might Mary's experience of Ta-Na-E-Ka have been different if she could not use a restaurant for food and shelter?

_____

_____

5. In your opinion, how might Meg explain the experiences of the Lins and the Gleasons as described in "The All-American Slurp"?

_____

_____

Paragraph

Rachel, the narrator of "Eleven," describes her upsetting experience at school. The only thing that cheers her up during the ordeal is remembering that her family will celebrate her birthday that evening. Think about what Rachel's birthday celebration with her family might have been like. Then, continue Rachel's story by telling about her birthday party.

_____

_____

_____

_____

_____

_____

_____

_____

_____

_____

Short Essay

Discovering one's true self

PREPARE TO WRITE. Each of the selections in this unit deals with how people learn who they truly are. Some of the characters have experiences that draw out their true selves. Use this chart to record the ways certain characters from the selections find out who they really are.

Character	Experience that changed him or her	What is discovered about true self
Matt Kaizer		
Mary Whitebird		
Narrator of "The All-American Slurp"		

WRITE. Choose one of the characters, and in two or three paragraphs, explain how the character changed and what experiences caused him or her to change.

_____

_____

_____

_____

_____

_____

_____

_____

_____

_____

_____

_____

_____

_____

_____

_____

_____

_____

_____

Supplemental
Activity Worksheets

ASSIGNMENT LOG

Date:

Subject:

Assignment:

Due date:

Date:

Subject:

Assignment:

Due date:

Date:

Subject:

Assignment:

Due date:

Date:

Subject:

Assignment:

Due date:

Date:

Subject:

Assignment:

Due date:

Date:

Subject:

Assignment:

Due date:

Date:

Subject:

Assignment:

Due date:

Date:

Subject:

Assignment:

Due date:

Name_____ Class_____ Date_____

READER'S JOURNAL

Date:_____

_____

_____

_____

_____

_____

_____

_____

_____

_____

_____

_____

_____

_____

_____

_____

_____

_____

_____

_____

_____

_____

_____

_____

_____

_____

_____

_____

_____

RESEARCH JOURNAL

Use this form as you work through a research project. As you get started researching, you may need to narrow or broaden your topic for research based on your initial findings.

Topic of study: _____

Narrower topic for research:_____

Hypotheses or predictions: _____

Possible sources (circle all of those you think will apply):

Books   Reference materials   Periodicals   Internet   Interview   Other

Initial findings:_____

_____

_____

_____

Notes about any relationships or patterns in your data:_____

_____

_____

_____

Notes from evaluating and interpreting your data: _____

_____

_____

_____

Conclusions you can make: _____

_____

_____

_____

Notes from exchanges of ideas with peers:_____

_____

_____

_____

Generalizations you can make about the topic: _____

_____

_____

_____

RESEARCH LOG

Your research journal, which could be a notebook or an electronic file, is a good place for taking notes on your topic and for documenting your sources. When you document a source, include the following:

- **author.** Write complete name(s) of author(s), editor (s) and translator(s).
- **title.** Write the full title exactly as it appears on the title page; include the edition if noted.
- **place of publication, publisher, date of publication.** Copy the publisher's name from the title page. Copy the place and date from the copyright page.
- **location and call number.** Note where you found the book. If it is from the library, write the call number.

1. Author: _____

   Title: _____

   Place, publisher, date: _____

   Location and call number: _____

2. Author: _____

   Title: _____

   Place, publisher, date: _____

   Location and call number: _____

3. Author: _____

   Title: _____

   Place, publisher, date: _____

   Location and call number: _____

4. Author: _____

   Title: _____

   Place, publisher, date: _____

   Location and call number: _____

5. Author: _____

   Title: _____

   Place, publisher, date: _____

   Location and call number: _____

6. Author: _____

   Title: _____

   Place, publisher, date: _____

   Location and call number: _____

INTERNET RESEARCH LOG

The Internet is a convenient research tool but it also presents some challenges. As you jump from one Internet site to another, it's easy to lose track of how you got from place to place. Mapping your navigation in your research journal is a good way to keep track of the sites you have visited and the information you found there.

```
┌─────────────┐     ┌─────────────┐     ┌─────────────┐     ┌─────────────────┐
│ topic of your│ →  │search engine │ →  │   keywords   │ →  │names/addresses of│
│   research   │    │    used      │    │ or phrases used│  │ sites you explore│
│              │    │              │    │  to search   │    │                 │
└─────────────┘     └─────────────┘     └─────────────┘     └─────────────────┘

┌─────────────┐     ┌─────────────┐     ┌──────────────────────────────┐
│names/addresses│ → │ new keywords │ →  │ complete documentation for sites│
│ of linked sites│  │ used to search│   │  you actually use for information│
│  you explore │    │              │    │                              │
└─────────────┘     └─────────────┘     └──────────────────────────────┘
```

Topic: _____

Search engine: _____

First keyword(s) or phrase tried: _____

Promising hits (site names/addresses): _____

_____

_____

_____

Links: _____

_____

_____

New keyword(s) or phrase tried: _____

Promising hits (titles of sources): _____

_____

_____

_____

Complete documentation for the two most promising sites: _____

_____

_____

Answer Key

"The Goodness of Matt Kaizer"

DAILY ORAL LANGUAGE

We're going there tomorrow.
"Did you see the way Karlyn looked at me?" Joyce cried.

SKILL BUILDERS

Vocabulary

1. beatable
2. rasping
3. admirable
4. biting
5. flushed
6. enjoyable
7. staring
8. fictional
9. climbable
10. presentable

Language, Grammar, and Style

Responses will vary.

SELECTION CHECK TEST 4.1.1

CHECKING YOUR READING

Short Answer

1. The gang calls Matt "Spirit."
2. Matt's father is a minister.
3. Mr. Bataky thinks Matt is an angel.
4. He dares him to go back.
5. He is clean and dresses neatly.

Vocabulary in Context

1. Marcel worked hard to maintain his **reputation** as a good student.
2. For weeks after Hannah got over her bronchitis infection, her voice remained **raspy.**
3. The winning team's faces were **flushed** with exertion.
4. Even though he knew he deserved his punishment, Randal was **sulky** the whole time he was on restriction.
5. The coach yelled at his players after he caught them **taunting** the other team.

READER'S TOOLBOX
Sentence Completion

1. **One-dimensional characters** are also called *flat characters* or *caricatures*.
2. The plot of a story centers on the main **conflict**.
3. The most important person or animal in a literary work is called the **main character**.
4. When a character faces a struggle within himself or herself, he or she is experiencing **internal conflict**.
5. **Three-dimensional characters** have many qualities, like real people do.

SELECTION TEST 4.1.2
"The Goodness of Matt Kaizer"

INSIGHTFUL READING
Matching

1. b
2. d
3. a
4. e
5. c

True or False

1. True
2. False
3. True
4. False
5. True

VOCABULARY IN CONTEXT

1. When the children heard the sound of the ice cream truck, they **bolted** out of the house.
2. In the scary movie I saw yesterday, the monster had a **ghastly** appearance.
3. The puppy fetched its leash and let out an **imploring** bark, indicating he wanted to go for a walk.
4. After his surgery, my father was slightly **delirious** from the medication.
5. The path we were following in the woods seemed to disappear, forcing us to **retreat** and find a new path.

UNDERSTANDING LITERARY CONCEPTS
Short Answer

1. Responses will vary, but students might note that Matt suffers internal conflict when he realizes that he is good inside after all. Also, Mr. Bataky faces external conflict as he fights liver disease and internal conflict as he struggles with his "bad life" when he is sick.
2. Students should explain that Matt Kaizer is a three-dimensional character because he has the complex qualities of a real human being. In other words, Matt seems like a real person.

CRITICAL WRITING

1. Cause and effect
   Responses will vary, but students might choose to focus on one of the following cause-effect relationships: Matt took pride in the fact that he never refused a dare causing him to accept his father's dare to help Mr. Bataky. Matt could not refuse the dare to help Mr. Bataky causing Mr. Bataky to feel better and Matt to change. Matt changed causing the dynamics of his group of friends to change.
2. Good deeds
   Responses will vary, but you might encourage students, either in writing or discussion, to draw parallels between their experience of helping someone and Matt's experience of helping Mr. Bataky.

SELECTION WORKSHEET 1.2 ANSWERS

"Eleven"

DAILY ORAL LANGUAGE

Have you ever been to the White House?
She doesn't want to grow older because she likes being a kid.

SKILL BUILDERS

Language, Grammar, and Style

1. Yesterday I went for a walk.
   Tomorrow I will go for a walk.
2. Yesterday Raymond was studying with me.
   Tomorrow Raymond will be studying with me.
3. Yesterday we were rehearsing.
   Tomorrow we will be rehearsing.
4. Yesterday I ate pizza.
   Tomorrow I will eat pizza.
5. Yesterday Mya taught biology.
   Tomorrow Mya will teach biology.
6. Yesterday Simon did run to the store.
   Tomorrow Simon will run to the store.
7. Yesterday Anna met Carrie at the library.
   Tomorrow Anna will meet Carrie at the library.
8. Yesterday Charlie was reading in front of the class.
   Tomorrow Charlie will be reading in front of the class.
9. Yesterday I saw Tristin.
   Tomorrow I will see Tristin.
10. Yesterday Melania was eating hot lunch.
    Tomorrow Melania will be eating hot lunch.

Vocabulary

Responses will vary.

SELECTION CHECK TEST 4.1.3

"Eleven"

CHECKING YOUR READING

Short Answer

1. You feel like you're still ten.
2. She makes her wear a red sweater.
3. She says it is ugly, with red plastic buttons, a collar, and stretched-out sleeves.
4. She has a birthday party to look forward to tonight.
5. She wished the day would be far away already.

READER'S TOOLBOX
Sentence Completion
1. A **simile** is a comparison using *like* or *as.*
2. Writers use **sensory details**, words or phrases that describe how things look, sound, smell, taste, or feel, to create description.
3. **Description** is a type of writing that portrays a character, object, or scene.
4. The phrase ". . . it's hanging all over the edge like a waterfall" is an example of **simile.**
5. Effective description contains precise **nouns, verbs, adjectives,** and **adverbs.**

SELECTION TEST 4.1.4
"Eleven"

INSIGHTFUL READING
Short Answer
1. Rachel's teacher makes Rachel wear a sweater that does not belong to her.
2. Student responses should reflect Rachel's explanation in the story: "Because she's older and the teacher, she's right and I'm not."
3. Rachel thinks that if she was one hundred and two, she would know how to tell Mrs. Price that the sweater was not hers.
4. Rachel remembers that her family will celebrate her birthday that night.
5. Another classmate remembers that the red sweater is hers.

UNDERSTANDING LITERARY CONCEPTS
Short Answer
1. A simile is a comparison using *like* or *as.* Student examples will vary. One example from "Eleven" is "the red sweater's still sitting there like a big red mountain."
2. Students may cite the words *eleven, not mine, Happy birthday, happy birthday to you.* Students might also recall that Cisneros repeats the numbers eleven through one repeatedly.
3. Students should note that the use of sensory details and precise nouns, verbs, adverbs, and adjectives help to create effective description.

CRITICAL WRITING
Choose ONE of the following prompts.
1. Your best birthday
Responses will vary, but encourage students to use "Eleven" as a model. You might have students compare their ideas about birthdays and growing older to Rachel's ideas expressed in "Eleven."
2. Summarize ideas
Students should explain Rachel's idea that, as you grow older, you still have all of your other previous ages inside of you. Students should also explain their opinion of Rachel's ideas and their own ideas about growing older.

SELECTION WORKSHEET 1.3 ANSWERS
"Why?"

DAILY ORAL LANGUAGE
Please tell your dog to lie down.
We saw the silliest movie last night.

SKILL BUILDERS

Language, Grammar, and Style

1. me; I
2. It; everything; they; everything
3. me; I; I; they
4. I; one
5. I; you; I
6. it; everyone; anything
7. I; everybody
8. it
9. it; one
10. you; it; nobody

Vocabulary

1. nervously
2. slowly
3. quietly
4. thoughtfully
5. strongly
6. hurriedly
7. obnoxiously
8. frequently
9. frightfully
10. frigidly

SELECTION CHECK TEST 4.1.5

"Why?"

CHECKING YOUR READING

Short Answer

1. Little children ask questions because they are unfamiliar with everything.
2. The word "why" taught Anne not only to ask but to think.
3. People would be more honest and good if they asked themselves "Why?" before they acted.
4. Both children and grownups hate to confess their faults and their bad side.
5. Punishment is ridiculous by the time a child reaches fourteen or fifteen.

VOCABULARY IN CONTEXT

1. Marcelle did the packing, because his wife was so **pedantic** that it took her forever.
2. Priscilla's **conscience** bothered her so badly that she confessed what she had done.
3. Benjamin Franklin is remembered for working hard to develop his **character**.

READER'S TOOLBOX

Matching

1. c
2. b
3. e

SELECTION TEST 4.1.6

"Why?"

INSIGHTFUL READING

True or False
1. False
2. True
3. False
4. False
5. True

VOCABULARY IN CONTEXT
1. Once the store manager understood that the customer's request was **reasonable**, he agreed to give her a refund.
2. My dad agreed to take us to the mall if we promised to stop **badgering** him about it.
3. Mateo's **conscience** told him that he shouldn't read his sister's journal, and he felt terrible after he did it.

UNDERSTANDING LITERARY CONCEPTS

Short Answer
1. A regular essay is nonfiction that expresses a writer's thoughts about a subject. A personal essay is an essay that relates to the life of the writer.
2. Personal essays are told from the writer's point of view (first-person point of view), using such words as *I* or *me.*
3. A thesis is the single idea, or main idea, that the entire essay works to develop. A good essay is organized into an introduction, a body, and a conclusion.

CRITICAL WRITING
1. Teaching children
   Students should identify Frank's main points, such as the ideas that children should ask questions to learn and parents should not be responsible for shaping a child's character. Students should explain whether they agree with these ideas and share their own opinions on how children should learn.
2. "Why?"
   Responses will vary, but students' poems should demonstrate creativity in responding to the questions provided. Evaluate students' work based on the content of their poem, rather than on the structure.

SELECTION WORKSHEET 1.4 ANSWERS

"Ta-Na-E-Ka"

DAILY ORAL LANGUAGE
There were a lot of geese at the lake.
"May I stay out an hour later tonight?" Peter asked.

SKILL BUILDERS

Language, Grammar, and Style
1. families: noun; reservation: noun
2. They: pronoun; now: adverb
3. and: conjunction; his: pronoun

4. Roger: noun; trembling: adjective
5. asks: verb; about: preposition
6. occurred: verb; Indian: noun
7. squooshy: adjective
8. but: conjunction; only: adverb
9. lost-and-found: adjective; said: verb
10. truth: noun; Hamburgers: noun
11. Argh: interjection; spat: verb
12. that: pronoun; for: preposition

Vocabulary

Responses will vary.

SELECTION CHECK TEST 4.1.7

"Ta-Na-E-Ka"

CHECKING YOUR READING

Short Answer

1. Ta-Na-E-Ka is a test of survival.
2. The author thought that the Kaw began the women's liberation movement.
3. She decides to spend it in the bathroom of Ernie's Riverside restaurant.
4. He was underweight, blistered, bloody, and had swollen, red eyes.
5. He had discovered a deer shot by soldiers and he ate it.

VOCABULARY IN CONTEXT

1. In a Buddhist marriage ceremony, the couple drinks from a **sacred** bowl.
2. "It's time to see if he can **fend** for himself," the ranger said as he let the eagle go.
3. Angela chose to investigate her family **heritage** for her research paper.
4. True courage is a **virtue** most of us don't know we have until it is tested in some way.
5. The townspeople extended warm **hospitality** to the refugees.

READER'S TOOLBOX

Short Answer

1. Responses will vary.
2. Responses will vary. Mary and her cousin Roger trained for Ta-Na-E-Ka, a survival test all 11-year-old Kaw girls and boys endure. Dreading the five nights alone in the forest, she forms a plan. Leaving home, she buys food at a riverside restaurant with money she's borrowed from her teacher and then later sneaks back in to sleep. The owner discovers her but allows her to stay. She returns home well-fed and clean. Her cousin Roger is bloody and blistered, but proud. Her relatives are angry when Mary tells her story, but soon her Grandfather praises her ingenuity and determines that she passed the test.

SELECTION TEST 4.1.8

"Ta-Na-E-Ka"

INSIGHTFUL READING

Multiple Choice

1. What does "Ta-Na-E-Ka" mean to the Kaw Indians?
   b. It is a coming-of-age endurance test.

2. Roger Deer Leg, Mary's cousin, wants to be _____ when he grows older.
   c. an accountant
3. The Kaw Indians are a subtribe of the _____.
   a. Sioux Nation
4. Mary and Roger were to spend _____ in the woods.
   b. 5 days
5. Mary spent her Ta-Na-E-Ka at _____.
   d. a restaurant

Short Answer

1. Grandfather still speaks the Kaw language, a Sioux dialect. He speaks English only with white men. Also, he requires his family members to experience Ta-Na-E-Ka, even though most of the other Kaw families gave up the old customs.
2. He taught them how to eat grasshoppers and showed them which berries to eat.
3. She borrowed it from her teacher. She promised her teacher that she would baby-sit for her ten times.
4. Ernie teaches Mary how to cook certain dishes, and Mary teaches Ernie many of the legends of the Kaw Indians.
5. The members of her family are not happy, but Grandfather admits that Mary's method of surviving Ta-Na-E-Ka was clever and that she would have survived under any conditions.

VOCABULARY IN CONTEXT

1. José was **dejected** when he learned that he did not get the lead role in the school play.
2. My classmates and I had **anticipated** our field trip to the museum for weeks, and we were not disappointed by it.
3. The woman involved in the shipwreck was on the TV news explaining how she survived the **ordeal**.
4. The **shrewd** businesswoman was successful because she was always able to find a solution to each problem she faced.
5. My sister looked at me with **hostility** when I told Mom that she was the one who broke the VCR.

UNDERSTANDING LITERARY CONCEPTS

Short Answer

1. Responses will vary, but students might say the dialogue demonstrated that Mary is a strong and confident character who is not afraid to stick up for her ideas. Grandfather respects the old customs of the Kaw, but he is wise enough to acknowledge that their people must adjust to the time in which they are living.
2. In a literary work, plot is a series of events related to a central conflict, or struggle.
3. Students should say that the central conflict in the selection revolves around the fact that Mary must find a way to survive Ta-Na-E-Ka even though she wishes she did not have to participate at all.

CRITICAL WRITING

1. Women's roles
   Responses will vary, but students should identify and address the information provided in the selection about the Kaw customs regarding women. (Most of this information can be found on text page 36.)
2. The plot to a sequel
   Responses will vary, but students should focus on demonstrating their understanding of Mary's character based on what they learn about her in "Ta-Na-E-Ka."

SELECTION WORKSHEET 1.5 ANSWERS

"The All-American Slurp"

DAILY ORAL LANGUAGE

Are you a Democrat or a Republican?
There are many things that I do not understand about America.

SKILL BUILDERS

Language, Grammar, and Style

Responses will vary.

Vocabulary

Responses will vary. Possible responses are given.
1. honor
2. go forward
3. liking
4. cool and dry
5. disorder

SELECTION CHECK TEST 4.1.9

"The All-American Slurp"

CHECKING YOUR READING

Short Answer

1. Mrs. Lin was reluctant to buy her daughter jeans.
2. The narrator's friend was Meg.
3. The narrator was embarrassed that others noticed her family slurping their soup.
4. He said she was a very stupid girl.
5. After chasing a pea around his plate with chopsticks, he eats it with his fingers.

VOCABULARY IN CONTEXT

1. The night was so **sultry** that we turned on every fan in the house.
2. Marcella liked many things about America, but she found fast food **revolting.**
3. When the teacher called out the questions, the whole class answered in **unison.**
4. After some **tense** moments, the Coast Guard ship pulled the survivor on board.
5. The team accused the coach of **favoritism** when he gave his son the best position.

READER'S TOOLBOX

Sentence Completion

1. **Onomatopoeia** is the use of words of phrases that sound like what they name.
2. A literary work may have several **themes.**
3. To **immigrate** means to *arrive and settle in a new country or region.*
4. The Lin family **emigrated** from China.
5. *Slurp, z-z-z-zip,* and *crunch* are examples of **onomatopoeia.**

"The All-American Slurp"

INSIGHTFUL READING

Sentence Completion
1. The Lin family came to the United States from **China**.
2. With the help of his new friends, the narrator's brother learned how to play **baseball** and earned a spot on his school team.
3. After the narrator rode a boy's bicycle, her mother agreed to buy **jeans** for her.
4. At the French restaurant, the narrator's family embarrassed her by slurping their **soup**.
5. After the Lins' dinner party, the narrator and Meg both get **(chocolate) milkshakes** from Dairy Queen.

Short Answer
1. The Lins learned that Americans eat raw celery with the strings. They also learned that Americans sometimes eat buffet style.
2. The fact that English verbs change tense fascinated Mr. Lin because Chinese verbs have no tense.
3. The family wanted to celebrate Father's promotion at a nice, expensive restaurant.
4. Chinese etiquette forced Mr. Lin to react this way.
5. Responses will vary, but students might suggest that the narrator was probably relieved to learn that Americans slurp, as her family had done in the expensive restaurant.

VOCABULARY IN CONTEXT
1. I was **mortified** to discover that I offended my guest by pronouncing his name incorrectly.
2. My mother told me to chew with my mouth closed, saying that I needed a lesson in proper **etiquette**.
3. My brother was recently hired at an **electronics** store, and he was learning a lot about radios and television sets.
4. Susan was **systematic** when doing her homework, always working on her math assignment first.
5. The football team created a **spectacle** at school the day they showed up in cheerleader's uniforms.

UNDERSTANDING LITERARY CONCEPTS

Multiple Choice
1. Which of the following words is an example of **onomatopoeia**?
   b. hiss
2. Which of the following sentences might be considered a **theme** of "The All-American Slurp"?
   d. People must be patient and understanding when learning the customs and etiquette of other cultures.

CRITICAL WRITING
1. Defining America
   Responses will vary. You might encourage students, either in writing or discussion, to compare their ideas of America to Lin family's ideas as expressed in the selection.
2. Using onomatopoeia
   Responses will vary but should demonstrate a basic understanding of the literary technique *onomatopoeia*. You might engage students in a discussion about the challenges of using onomatopoeia effectively, touching on Lensey Namioka's use of the technique in "The All-American Slurp."

VOCABULARY WORKSHEET

Spelling
1. disgrace
   c. discrace
2. favoritism
   b. favoratism
3. mortified
   b. mordified
4. conscience
   a. consciense
5. audacity
   d. audasity

Synonyms
1. Matt Kaizer was <u>dejected</u> when he learned that he was good inside.
   a. depressed
2. The Lin family slowly learned American <u>etiquette</u>.
   c. manners
3. Roger's parents could not hide their <u>hostility</u> for Mary when she returned home.
   a. ill will
4. Mary had to be very <u>shrewd</u> in order to survive Ta-Na-E-Ka.
   d. clever
5. Rachel might have been afraid her classmates would <u>taunt</u> her for wearing such an ugly red sweater.
   c. tease

Antonyms
1. Matt's experience with Mr. Bataky put him in a <u>sulky</u> mood.
   a. cheerful
2. Anne Frank believes children <u>badger</u> adults with questions because the children want to learn more.
   d. delight
3. The narrator of "The All-American Slurp" was <u>mortified</u> when her family slurped soup at the expensive restaurant.
   a. proud
4. Matt's friends wanted Matt to tell them all of Mr. Bataky's <u>ghastly</u> stories.
   b. comforting
5. The Lins thought sour cream was a <u>revolting</u> food because they were not used to dairy products.
   d. appealing

Sentence Completion
1. During her Ta-Na-E-Ka, Mary accepted the **hospitality** offered by Ernie.
2. The Lins shook their heads in **unison** when they were offered sour cream.
3. I hope Rachel's **ordeal** with the red sweater did not ruin her birthday celebration at home.
4. Matt had a **reputation** for being the "baddest of the bad."
5. Anne Frank believes that a child's **conscience** will punish them if they act improperly.

READER'S TOOLBOX
1. **Onomatopoeia** is the use of words or phrases that sound like what they name.
2. In a **personal essay,** a writer expresses his or her thoughts about a subject that relates his or her life.
3. A comparison using *like* or *as* is called a **simile.**
4. **Conflict** is a struggle between two people or things in a literary work.
5. A **theme** is a central idea in a literary work.

QUESTIONS FOR WRITING, DISCUSSION, AND RESEARCH

1. Responses will vary. For example, students might choose Mary Whitebird's experience with her Ta-Na-E-Ka and explain that both she and Matt Kaizer did something they didn't want to do. Mary learned that she was shrewd and brave, and Matt learned that he was good inside.
2. Responses will vary. For example, students might focus on Matt Kaizer's attempts to impress his friends by being "gross" or "the baddest of the bad." They might choose Rachel and explain that her desire to be accepted probably led to her being so upset about having to wear the red sweater.

UNIT TEST ANSWERS

INSIGHTFUL READING

Matching

1. b
2. a
3. d
4. a
5. c

True or False

1. True
2. False
3. False
4. True
5. False

VOCABULARY IN CONTEXT

Sentence Completion

1. My mother always tells me that honesty is a **virtue** that will help me make many friends.
2. Katrina's face was **flush** when she read her speech in front of the entire school body.
3. I think the candidate **disgraced** himself during the debate by insulting his opponent.
4. My parents do not show **favoritism** because they treat me and my siblings equally.
5. The two boxers **leered** at each other as they entered the boxing ring.

UNDERSTANDING LITERARY CONCEPTS

Short Answer

1. Onomatopoeia is the use of words or phrases that sound like what they name. Examples from the selection include *shloop, zip,* and *slurp*.
2. "Why?" by Anne Frank is a personal essay.
3. Responses will vary. Possible responses: Mr. Bataky did not want to die without confessing the bad things he had done in his life. Matt did not want to visit Mr. Bataky again, but his father dared him.
4. "Eleven" uses several similes to describe growing old.
5. Responses will vary. Possible responses might include "Stand up for what you believe in" or "Respect your cultural heritage."

CRITICAL WRITING

Short Answer

1. Students might explain that after Matt heard about the story of a man who truly lived a "bad" life, he realized that he was not bad. They might also suggest that, by helping Mr. Bataky feel better, Matt realized that he could do goodness.
2. Students might suggest that Rachel is shy and lacking in self-confidence. They might also note that Rachel respects authority.

3. Anne Frank expresses her thoughts about a subject that relates to her life. She uses the pronouns *I* and *me.*
4. Responses will vary. Students might suggest that Mary would have had to spend her Ta-Na-E-Ka as Roger did. Others might suggest that Mary would have thought of another clever idea to make her challenge easier to survive.
5. Responses will vary. Students might suggest that Meg seems more easy-going than the narrator and might just explain what happened at the dinner parties. Others might suggest that readers would not learn about the struggles of the Lin family because Meg does not seem to notice.

Paragraph

Responses will vary, but students should demonstrate a clear understanding of Rachel's character based on the ideas and emotions she shares with the audience in her narration of "Eleven."

Short Essay

Discovering one's true self
Responses will vary depending on the character students choose to focus on. Students should demonstrate a thorough understanding of the character they choose by clearly stating how the character changed and by explaining what experiences caused him or her to change.